8 BROADS IN THE KITCHEN

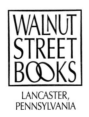

Desserts!

8 superb chefs share their favorite
cakes, pies, bars, cookies, cobblers,
crisps, and candies

WALNUT
STREET
BOOKS

LANCASTER,
PENNSYLVANIA

walnutstreetbooks.com

Acknowledgments

As the African proverb wisely states, "It takes a village." The 8 Broads in the Kitchen are especially grateful to our village. We couldn't have created this cookbook without those of you we include here.

Kudos to our photographers for their exceptional support and creative talent in bringing our desserts to life: Karen Segraves, KES Photography; Mark Smith and Matthew Lovette, Jumping Rocks Photography; Christian Gianelli, Christian Gianelli Photography; and Jenna Strawbridge.

We so appreciate Joan and Dane Wells, Larie Engles, Dani Hanscom Thode, and Kristie Rosset, who let us mess up their kitchens for photo shoots, as well as those who housed us during photo shoots—Larie Engles and Linda Hill.

A special thank you to our friends, families, neighbors, and guests across the country, who generously offered to test our recipes and often suggested ways to improve them.

A big Broad hug to all of you: Jenny Anderson, Katie Arthur, Carol Baxter, Shelby Book, Jan Bowdon, Rachel Brown, Mert Brubaker, Debbie Burke, Marion Campbell, Cathie Canon, Jeff Cook, Peter Chenaux, Rob Chenaux, Larie Engles, Tim and Lisa Engles, Elaine Gerwig, Mary Griggs, Linda Hill, Joanna Huacani, Rose Lansing, Jim Leitch, Rebecca Bliss Lilley, Esther Link, Janet Lowenstein, Roger Lund, Robin Lunger, Wayne Lunger, Debbie Merritt, Susan Manicke, Pat Marinelli, Debbie McCord, Kelsey Morrison, Stacey and Jarod Mundt, Ruthellen Ondrus, Mehrvash Poole, Steve Poole, Amanda Benins Potter, Lori Powell, Linda Den Riddler, Janice Riley, Ray Rosset, Amanda Sandoz, Matt Sautter, Rita Scardino, Mike Schen, Julie Katz Schoper, Sally Shakleford, Jeff Steinberg, Abbey Stohs, Les Stohs, Anna Takrouri, Brooklyn Theodore, Abby and Dustin Tumbale, Kandace Van Gorder, Care Wacker, Erma Weaver, Joan Wells, Kelly Wilde, Tiffany Wilson, and Mirjam Zimmerman!

Design by Cliff Snyder

Desserts!

Copyright © 2019 by 8 Broads in the Kitchen

Softcover: 9781947597242; PDF: 9781947597259; EPUB: 9781947597266; Kindle: 9781947597273

Library of Congress Control Number: Data available.

Desserts! is published by Walnut Street Books, Lancaster, Pennsylvania
info@walnutstreetbooks.com

To our families, our friends, and our guests—

For all the times we said, "Here, try this!"
and you loved what you tasted, thank you!

And for those times that you didn't quite love what
we made, thank you for encouraging us to keep trying!

Table of Contents

A Word About Our Ingredients

Blind bake: To bake a pie crust or other pastry without its filling. A pastry should be blind baked completely if its filling doesn't need to be baked. A pastry should be partially blind baked if its filling requires less baking time than the crust. To prevent an empty crust from shrinking as it bakes, cover the bottom of the crust with foil, and then top it with pie weights, or their equivalent, before blind baking.

Brown sugar: Light brown, unless otherwise noted.

Butter: Unsalted. (We do not recommend margarine because it doesn't produce the same high-quality result, and it just isn't good for you.)

Confectioners sugar: Often referred to as powdered sugar, icing sugar, frosting sugar, or 10x sugar.

Eggs: Large, unless otherwise noted. We recommend that when cooking for pregnant, auto-immune-challenged people, and small children, you use pasteurized eggs. Use these eggs especially in recipes that call for overnight storage before cooking or baking, as well as for custards that do not cook at high temperatures for longer periods of time. You can find pasteurized eggs in the dairy section of your grocery store.

Flour: Unbleached and all-purpose, unless otherwise noted.

Lukewarm water: Warm, but under 110° so it doesn't kill yeast.

Oats: May be quick-cooking oats, but never instant. Or if a recipe calls for rolled oats, they need to be *rolled* oats, not quick or instant.

Oil: Canola, rapeseed, or corn oil, unless we specify olive oil.

Salt: Table salt, kosher salt, and sea salt can be used interchangeably, but we suggest using the recommended salt if specified. All are sodium chloride, and all are used for flavor. It's really a matter of preference. Kosher salt and sea salt come in both coarse and fine grains. Because fine grain kosher salt, or fine grain sea salt, incorporates better, we recommend using them for baking and cooking. But since sea salt is expensive, we recommend using it for finishing, as in sea salted caramel chocolates or cookies.

Sugar: Granulated, unless otherwise noted.

Size matters! Use the size pans the recipe calls for. Other sizes will give different results. For example, a 9-inch pie crust holds 1½ times the amount of filling that an 8-inch pie crust holds.

Also, by the 8 Broads—
Breakfast and Brunch Recipes
(see page 256 for more details)

Our Journey Together

8 Broads in the Kitchen officially came into being in 2008. But that event was part of eight individual journeys that began many years earlier, as each of us in our own way discovered the joy and friendship that comes from sharing good food with family and friends.

Who could have foreseen that eight women from totally different backgrounds and cultures would meet, form friendships stronger than steel, and collaborate in an enterprise that has resulted in three published cookbooks.

From the humble origin of a food blog intended to offer our most requested recipes, our collaboration as 8 Broads has encouraged us all to grow professionally and personally.

We share a common food philosophy and commitment—that we use the best and freshest ingredients, ones that are sourced locally, prepared with love, and shared with friends.

Innkeeping was one common thread that brought us together and still plays a large role in our lives. Our bed and breakfasts have been scattered across the United States, from the East Coast to the West Coast, and points between. We have accumulated over 200 years of combined innkeeping experience, having served hundreds of thousands of breakfasts to

enthusiastic guests, and baked enough cookies to pave all the roads between us.

While we do less innkeeping today, we continue to share our passion for food as we teach food classes and do food consulting.

This cookbook is personal. We delved into old family recipes, childhood favorites, and recipes our mothers and grandmothers made. We squinted to read faded, hand-written notes scribbled on the backs of envelopes. We reminisced about growing up in Switzerland, Scotland, and Canada. We baked, tested, adapted, tasted, laughed, and swooned. We rediscovered, as we shared these recipes, that desserts are comfort food, meant to be shared.

As Erma Bombeck once said, "Seize the moment. Remember all those women on the Titanic who waved off the dessert cart."

Bars & Squares
No Matter How You Slice It

These squares are Houdinis.
Serve them and watch them disappear!

Bars & Squares, No Matter How You Slice It

Apricot Orange Shortbread Bars

ELLEN GUTMAN CHENAUX

Makes 16 squares

Prep Time: 20-30 minutes ❧ *Baking Time: 1 hour*

1 cup apricot preserves

1 Tablespoon orange liqueur

16 Tablespoons (2 sticks) unsalted butter, softened

¾ cup sugar

1 teaspoon almond extract

2 cups flour

¼ teaspoon salt

¼ cup crumbled almond paste

½ cup sliced almonds, *divided*

1. Preheat the oven to 325°.
2. In a small bowl, blend together the preserves and liqueur. Set aside.
3. Grease an 8- or 9-inch square pan, including up the sides. Line the pan, including the sides, with parchment paper. Grease the parchment paper.
4. In an electric mixer, beat the butter and sugar together. Beat in the almond extract. Add the flour and salt and beat until just blended.
5. To make the topping, place 1 cup of the dough in a small bowl. Add the crumbled almond paste and combine with your fingers until you have formed small clumps. Mix in ¼ cup almonds. Set aside.
6. Pat the remaining dough evenly over the bottom of the square pan, pressing it down.
7. Spread the preserves mixture over the dough.
8. Using your fingertips, drop the topping over the preserves. Sprinkle the top with the remaining almonds, gently pressing down on the topping.
9. Bake for about 1 hour. The shortbread should be golden brown. Cool completely on a wire rack.
10. Lift the shortbread from the pan using the parchment paper. When completely cool, cut into 16 squares.

The Tartiest Lemon Bars Ever!

ELLEN GUTMAN CHENAUX

Makes 12 bars

Prep Time: 15-20 minutes ✂ *Baking Time: 35-45 minutes*

16 Tablespoons (2 sticks) unsalted butter, softened to room temperature

⅔ cup confectioners sugar, plus more for dusting the baked bars

2¼ cups flour, *divided*

2 cups sugar

4 large eggs

¼ cup freshly grated lemon zest (from about 3 lemons)

lemon juice and pulp (from the 3 lemons)

1 teaspoon baking powder

¼ cup flour

1. Preheat the oven to 350°. Grease a 9 × 13-inch baking pan.
2. Using an electric or hand mixer, beat the butter in a large bowl until fluffy.
3. Beat in the confectioners sugar.
4. Add 2 cups of flour, 1 cup at a time. Beat until moist clumps form.
5. Spoon the batter into the prepared baking pan. Press the dough (using a fork or spoon) over the bottom.
6. Bake until the crust is lightly golden, about 15 minutes.
7. While the crust is baking, beat the sugar and eggs in a medium bowl until blended.
8. Beat in the lemon zest, lemon juice, pulp, and baking powder. Then add the remaining ¼ cup flour.
9. Pour the filling over the hot crust, being careful not to jostle the baking pan when putting it in the oven. Bake until the center is set and the filling begins to brown, about 20-30 minutes.
10. Transfer the pan to a rack and cool completely. Refrigerate until you're ready to serve. Then cut the pastry into 12 bars. Transfer to a serving platter. Dust with additional confectioners sugar.

Tip: You can make these bars a day ahead. Just cover and refrigerate until you're ready to serve them. Then proceed as stated above.

Bars & Squares, No Matter How You Slice It

Lemon Cheese Bars

YVONNE MARTIN

Makes 48 1½-inch squares

Prep Time: 20 minutes ❧ *Baking Time: 30 minutes*

2 cups flour

1¾ cups sugar, *divided*

2 teaspoons baking powder

½ teaspoon salt

3 eggs, *divided*

½ cup canola oil

12 oz. (1½ 8-oz. packages) cream cheese, softened

zest and juice from 1 lemon

1. Preheat the oven to 350°. Lightly spray a 9 × 13-inch baking pan with non-stick coating.
2. Mix the flour, 1¼ cups sugar, baking powder, and salt in a medium bowl.
3. In a separate bowl, beat 2 of the eggs with the canola oil. Pour over flour mixture and combine. It should be quite crumbly.
4. Reserve a heaping cup of this mixture. Press the rest into the bottom of the baking pan. Bake at 350° for 15 minutes.
5. Beat the cream cheese with the remaining egg and ½ cup sugar. Beat in the lemon zest and lemon juice.
6. Spread the cream cheese-lemon mixture over the hot crust. Sprinkle remaining crumbs evenly over top. Bake for another 15 minutes, or until golden brown.
7. Cool and cut into 1½-inch squares.

These bars are like a cheesecake sandwich—with creamy lemon cheesecake sandwiched between layers of sugar cookie dough.

This is a perfect recipe for summer
when blueberries are plentiful.

Bars & Squares, No Matter How You Slice It

Blueberry Lemon Bars

LYNNETTE SCOFIELD

Makes 16 bars

Prep Time: 20 minutes ❧ *Baking Time: 25 minutes*

Crust

1½ cups graham cracker crumbs

6 Tablespoons (¾ stick) butter, melted

¼ cup sugar

zest from 1 lemon (reserve lemon juice for filling)

Filling

2 large egg yolks

14-ounce can sweetened condensed milk

½ cup fresh lemon juice

zest from a second lemon

1 cup fresh blueberries, *divided*

1. Preheat the oven to 350°. Spray an 8-inch square baking pan with non-stick spray. Set aside.
2. In a bowl, combine the cracker crumbs, melted butter, sugar, and lemon zest. Stir until crumbs are moist. Press the crumbs into the prepared pan, working them slightly up the side of the pan.
3. Bake the crust for 10 minutes. Remove from the oven and cool.
4. Meanwhile, mix the filling. Combine the egg yolks and condensed milk in a bowl. Stir in the lemon juice and lemon zest. Stir until the mixture is smooth and begins to thicken slightly.
5. Gently fold in most of the blueberries, reserving some for the top.
6. Pour the lemon mixture evenly over the baked crust and arrange the remaining blueberries on top.
7. Bake for 15 minutes or just until set.
8. Cool completely and then refrigerate until cold throughout. Then cut them into 9 big squares, and cut the squares diagonally in half to create 18 triangles for some visual interest.

Peach Bars

DANIELLE HANSCOM THODE

Makes 16 bars

Prep Time: 20 minutes ❧ *Baking Time: 45 minutes*

2¼ cups flour

1 cup sugar

16 Tablespoons (2 sticks) unsalted butter, at room temperature

1 cup chopped pecans

¼ teaspoon salt

½ teaspoon freshly grated nutmeg

1 large egg, beaten, at room temperature

8-10 oz. peach jam, homemade if you have it

1. Preheat oven to 350°. Spray an 8- or 9-inch square glass baking dish with non-stick spray.
2. Place all the ingredients except the peach jam in the mixing bowl of a stand mixer. Beat on low until crumbly.
3. Set aside 1½ cups of the crumb mixture.
4. Pat the remaining crumb mixture onto the bottom of the prepared baking dish.
5. Top with peach jam, leaving ½ inch of space uncovered to the edges.
6. Crumble reserved crumb mixture over the top of the jam.
7. Bake for approximately 45 minutes. Check after 35 minutes. If the top is getting too dark, cover with a piece of aluminum foil.
8. When the crumbs are golden brown, remove the pan from the oven. Cool completely before cutting into bars.

Brampton was once a peach plantation. The peach trees are all long gone, but we do like to offer peach treats every day during the growing season at the inn.

Fruit & Nut Energy Squares

KRISTIE ROSSET

Makes 16 squares

Prep Time: 15 minutes   Baking Time: 35-40 minutes

¼ cup, plus 2 Tablespoons, whole wheat flour

¼ teaspoon baking soda

¼ teaspoon salt

¼ teaspoon baking powder

¼ cup, plus 2 Tablespoons, dark brown sugar, packed

2 cups chopped walnut pieces

1 cup chopped dried apricots

¾ cup dried cranberries

¾ cup dried cherries, *or* blueberries

1 large egg

½ teaspoon vanilla

1. Preheat oven to 325°. Coat the interior of an 8-inch square baking pan with non-stick spray.
2. Whisk together in a large bowl the flour, baking soda, salt, baking powder, and brown sugar. Mix thoroughly. Add the walnuts and dried fruit. Mix the ingredients with your fingers until all the fruit and walnut pieces are coated with the dry mixture.
3. In a separate small bowl, whisk the egg with the vanilla until slightly thickened. Using a spatula, thoroughly scrape the egg into the fruit/flour bowl. Once again, mix with your fingers until all of the fruit and nuts are coated with the batter. Spread into the prepared pan.
4. Bake 35-40 minutes until golden brown.
5. Allow to cool. Then cut into 16 squares.

This delicious and nutritions snack was created as a packable, easy, energy bar for a two-day overnight kayaking trip on breathtaking Lake Ouachita in Arkansas. We paddled over 20 miles and slept on an island. It was a fabulous experience, and everyone loved the squares.

Indiana Mint Bars

YVONNE MARTIN

Makes 32 squares

Prep Time: 20 minutes ✻ Baking Time: 30 minutes ✻ Cooling Time: 30 minutes

1 cup flour

1 cup sugar

1½ cups chocolate syrup

4 eggs

8 Tablespoons butter (1 stick), softened to room temperature

8 Tablespoons butter (1 stick), softened to room temperature

1 Tablespoon milk

½ teaspoon peppermint extract

2 cups confectioners sugar

green food coloring

4 Tablespoons (half a stick) butter

1 cup chocolate chips, *or* 8 oz. semisweet chocolate chips

1. Preheat the oven to 350°. Grease a 9 × 13-inch baking pan with butter or cooking spray.
2. With an electric mixer, beat together the flour, sugar, chocolate syrup, eggs, and 8 Tablespoons butter until well combined.
3. Pour into the prepared pan. Bake for about 30 minutes, or until the top springs back when touched. Remove from the oven and let cool.
4. Meanwhile, begin the mint layer by beating together 8 Tablespoons butter, milk, peppermint extract, and confectioners sugar.
5. Add the green food coloring a couple drops at a time until you have the shade of green you like. I recommend a pale green, rather than a St. Patrick's green.
6. Spread the mint layer over the cooled brownies.
7. Make the chocolate topping by melting 4 Tablespoons of butter and chocolate chips together in a microwave-safe dish. Cook on high for 15-second intervals, stirring after each interval so you see when the chocolate has melted.
8. Pour the melted mixture over the mint layer, spreading carefully with a spatula if necessary.
9. Refrigerate until firm. Then cut into 32 squares.

Bars & Squares, No Matter How You Slice It

This recipe was given to me years ago by a friend.
I'm not sure why they are known as Indiana Mint Bars,
but they've been popular in Ohio as well!

Chocolate Cream Cheese Bars

LYNNETTE SCOFIELD

Makes 48 bars

Prep Time: 15 minutes ❦ *Baking Time: 25 minutes* ❦ *Icing Time: 10 minutes*

8 Tablespoons butter (1 stick), softened to room temperature

4 ounces cream cheese (half an 8-oz. package), softened to room temperature

1 cup sugar

3 eggs

2 teaspoons vanilla

1 cup flour

6 Tablespoons unsweetened cocoa powder

½ teaspoon baking soda

1½ cups semisweet chocolate chips, *divided*

⅓ cup sour cream, *divided*

1. Preheat the oven to 350°.
2. In a medium bowl, using an electric mixer, beat together the butter and cream cheese until well blended.
3. Add the sugar, eggs, and vanilla, and beat until blended.
4. In a separate bowl, use a whisk to blend the flour, cocoa powder, and baking soda. Add the flour mixture to the cream cheese mixture and blend.
5. Stir the 1 cup chocolate chips into the batter with a rubber spatula.
6. Spread the batter into a greased 9 × 13-inch baking dish. Bake for about 25 minutes, or until a cake tester inserted into the center comes out clean. Do not overbake. Allow to cool in the pan.
7. To make the icing, place the semisweet chocolate chips in a bowl and melt over a saucepan filled with hot, not boiling, water.
8. Remove from heat and add the sour cream in three additions, stirring well after each addition.
9. This will produce a thin layer of frosting for the bars. When the bars are cool, spread with frosting.
10. Cut into 48 bars.

Old-Fashioned Chocolate Sheet Squares

KRISTIE ROSSET

Makes 24 squares

Prep Time: 30 minutes ✿ *Baking Time: 20 minutes*

2 cups flour

2 cups sugar

½ teaspoon salt

16 Tablespoons (2 sticks) butter

1 cup water

¼ cup unsweetened cocoa powder

½ cup buttermilk

2 eggs, beaten

1 teaspoon baking soda

1 teaspoon vanilla

8 Tablespoons (1 stick) butter

3 Tablespoons unsweetened cocoa powder

6 Tablespoons milk

3¼ cups confectioners sugar

1 cup chopped pecans

1 teaspoon vanilla

dash of salt

1. Preheat the oven to 350°. Grease and flour an 11 × 16 × 1-inch jelly roll (rimmed baking sheet) pan.
2. Whisk the flour, sugar, and ½ teaspoon salt together in a large bowl (not plastic).
3. Combine the 16 Tablespoons butter, water, and ¼ cup cocoa powder in a medium saucepan. Bring to a boil over medium-high heat, stirring frequently. Pour over the flour mixture and stir.
4. Add the buttermilk, eggs, baking soda, and 1 teaspoon vanilla to the batter, whisking until smooth.
5. Pour the batter into the prepared pan.
6. Bake for 20 minutes.
7. While the cake bakes, make the icing. Combine 8 Tablespoons butter, 3 Tablespoons cocoa powder, and milk in a medium saucepan. Bring to a boil.
8. Remove the saucepan from the heat and add the confectioners sugar, nuts, 1 teaspoon vanilla, and dash of salt. Stir well until smooth.
9. Spread the icing over the hot cake immediately after taking it out of the oven. Then allow to cool completely before cutting.

Tri-Colored Squares

YVONNE MARTIN

Makes 36 squares

Prep Time: 30 minutes ❧ *Baking Time: 30-35 minutes* ❧ *Cooling Time: 45-60 minutes*

single crust pie crust
(see recipe on pages 200-201,
or use a store-bought crust)

¼ cup raspberry preserves

8 Tablespoons (1 stick) butter,
softened to room temperature

⅔ cup sugar

2 eggs, added one at a time

⅓ cup rice flour

⅔ cup flour

¼ teaspoon salt

red and green food coloring

4 Tablespoons (half a stick)
butter, melted

1½ cups confectioners sugar

1 teaspoon almond extract

1-2 Tablespoons milk

1. Preheat oven to 375°.
2. Roll out the pie crust to a 9-inch square and press into the bottom of an ungreased 9-inch square baking pan.
3. Spread raspberry preserves over the pie crust. Refrigerate while you make the batter.
4. Using an electric mixer, beat 8 Tablespoons of butter with ⅔ cup of sugar. Beat in the eggs, one at a time. Stir in the rice flour, flour, and salt.
5. Divide the batter into two equal portions. Using the food coloring, tint one portion pink and the other green. Spoon out by teaspoons on top of the raspberry preserves, alternating colors to give a checkerboard effect.
6. Bake for 15 minutes. Then reduce heat to 350° and continue baking for another 15-20 minutes, or until the cake springs back when touched.
7. Make the frosting by creaming together 4 Tablespoons butter, confectioners sugar, almond extract, and milk. Add more milk if needed to reach a spreading consistency. Spread over cooled cake.
8. Allow frosting to set. Then cut into 36 squares.

Turtle Squares

KRISTIE ROSSET

Makes 20 squares

Prep Time: 20 minutes ❧ *Baking Time: 18-22 minutes*

2 cups flour

2⅓ cups brown sugar,
lightly packed, *divided*

8 Tablespoons (1 stick)
butter, softened

1 cup coarsely
chopped pecans

13⅓ Tablespoons (2 sticks
plus 5⅓ Tablespoons) butter

1 cup chocolate chips

1. Preheat oven to 350°.
2. Combine the flour, 1 cup brown sugar and 8 Tablespoons butter in a food processor, or in a large bowl, using a pastry cutter to make fine crumbs.
3. Press crumbs firmly into a greased 9 × 13-inch baking pan. Sprinkle with pecans.
4. In a small saucepan over medium heat, cook 13⅓ Tablespoons butter and 1⅓ cups brown sugar together, stirring constantly until the entire surface boils. Boil for one minute. Then pour the mixture over the crust.
5. Bake for 18-22 minutes, until the surface is bubbly.
6. Remove from the oven and immediately sprinkle with chocolate chips. Allow the chips to melt for a moment, then swirl and spread over the entire base.
7. Cool before cutting into squares.

Easy, yummy treat that satisfies every sweet tooth!

Blondies, Brunettes, and Redheads

Peanut Butter Blondies of Insane Greatness

ELLEN GUTMAN CHENAUX

Makes 12-16 blondies

Prep Time: 20 minutes *Baking Time: 25-30 minutes*

1 cup flour

¼ cup cake flour

¾ teaspoon baking powder

⅛ teaspoon salt

⅓ cup smooth peanut butter

8 Tablespoons (1 stick) unsalted butter, melted and cooled til warm (not hot)

1 cup brown sugar

1 large egg

1 large egg yolk

1 teaspoon vanilla

¾ cup mini peanut butter cups (Trader Joe's has great ones)

¾ cup peanut butter chips

¼ cup semisweet chocolate chips

1. Preheat the oven to 350°.
2. Grease an 8 × 8-inch baking pan. Line it with parchment paper that overhangs the sides.
3. Mix together the flours, baking powder, and salt. Set aside.
4. In a medium-sized mixing bowl, mix together the peanut butter and melted butter. Whisk in the brown sugar, egg, egg yolk, and vanilla.
5. Mix in the flour mixture. Stir in the peanut butter cups and chips. The dough will be thick and chunky.
6. Scrape the dough into the prepared pan and spread it out evenly.
7. Bake for 25-30 minutes until the blondies are set and golden. Cool on a wire rack.
8. Then cut into squares.

I never liked blondies until I tried this recipe. Now I'm a believer!

Cookie Dough Brownies

KRISTIE ROSSET

Makes 16 brownies

Prep Time: 35 minutes ❧ *Baking Time: 30 minutes* ❧ *Chilling Time: 2 hours*

2 cups sugar

1½ cups flour

½ cup unsweetened
cocoa powder

½ teaspoon salt

4 eggs

1 cup vegetable oil

2 teaspoons vanilla

8 Tablespoons (1 stick)
butter, softened to
room temperature

½ cup brown sugar,
lightly packed

¼ cup sugar

2 Tablespoons milk

1 teaspoon vanilla

1 cup flour

1 cup semisweet, *or*
milk chocolate chips

1 Tablespoon butter

1. Preheat the oven to 350°. Grease a 9 × 13-inch baking pan with non-stick spray.
2. Combine the 2 cups sugar, 1½ cups flour, cocoa powder, and salt in the bowl of a stand mixer.
3. Add the eggs, oil, and 2 teaspoons vanilla. Beat at medium speed for 3 minutes.
4. Pour into the prepared pan. Bake for 30 minutes. Remove from oven and set on wire rack.
5. Cool completely.
6. Meanwhile, make the cookie dough by creaming the 8 Tablespoons butter, brown sugar, and ¼ cup sugar in a stand mixer.
7. Add the milk and 1 teaspoon vanilla and mix well.
8. Beat in the 1 cup flour on medium speed until thoroughly incorporated.
9. Spread over the cooled brownies. Chill for an hour or until firm.
10. Make a glaze by melting the chocolate chips and 1 Tablespoon butter in the microwave in 15-second intervals, stirring after each time, just until melted. Then spread over cooled brownies.
11. Refrigerate until ready to serve. Then cut into 16 squares.

This brownie satisfies the cookie dough lovers of the world, without the raw eggs!

Stout Brownies

DEBBIE MOSIMANN

Makes 12 brownies

Prep Time: 30 minutes ❧ *Baking Time: 25-30 minutes*

8 Tablespoons (1 stick) butter, melted until browned

¾ cup sugar

½ cup brown sugar

3 eggs, *divided*

6 oz. semisweet chocolate chips

⅓ cup stout beer

¾ cup flour

1 teaspoon salt

¼ cup unsweetened cocoa powder

1 cup coarsely broken walnuts, gently toasted and cooled

1. Preheat the oven to 350°.
2. Butter and flour an 8 × 8-inch baking pan, preferably metal.
3. In a bowl, mix the melted, browned butter and the two sugars.
4. Add the eggs, one at a time. Combine all well.
5. Melt chocolate chips with the beer in top of a double boiler. Then add to the above ingredients.
6. Mix the flour, salt, cocoa powder, and cooled, roasted walnut pieces in another bowl. Then add to the liquid ingredients. Mix together.
7. Pour into the prepared baking pan.
8. Bake for at least 25 minutes. Check carefully because they may need to bake longer. But don't over-bake them. They are finished when a little bit of batter still clings to the tester.
9. Cool, and then cut to serve.

Blondies, Brunettes, and Redheads

Karen, a long-time guest, shared this recipe with me, knowing how much I enjoy a glass of dark beer. I use a bourbon barrel-aged stout from a local brewery.

Blondies, Brunettes, and Redheads

White Chocolate Brownies

LYNNETTE SCOFIELD

Makes 9 large, or 18 bite-size, brownies
Prep Time: 10 minutes ❧ *Baking Time: 30 minutes*

8 Tablespoons (1 stick) unsalted butter

8 ounces white chocolate chips, *divided*

2 eggs

pinch of salt

½ cup sugar

½ teaspoon vanilla extract

½ teaspoon salt

1 cup flour

1¼ cups semisweet chocolate chips

1. Preheat the oven to 350°. Lightly grease an 8-inch square baking dish.
2. Melt the butter in a small saucepan over low heat. Remove the pan from the heat and add half the white chocolate chips. Do not stir.
3. Using an electric mixer, beat the eggs and a pinch of salt until frothy. Gradually add the sugar and beat until the mixture becomes pale yellow, and a slowly-dissolving ribbon forms when the beater is lifted.
4. Add the white chocolate mixture, vanilla, ½ teaspoon salt, and flour, mixing until just combined.
5. Stir in the semisweet chocolate chips and remaining white chocolate chips.
6. Bake for 30 minutes. Cool before cutting.

We have been making these since our Inn opened in 1999.
Is it the chocolate? The butter? You decide!

Apple Orange Brownies

LYNNETTE SCOFIELD

Makes 12 brownies

Prep Time: 15 minutes ✀ *Baking Time: 15 minutes*

6 Tablespoons (¾ stick) unsalted butter

1 cup brown sugar

½ cup applesauce

1 teaspoon grated orange zest

1 egg, beaten

1 teaspoon vanilla

1¼ cups flour, sifted

1 teaspoon baking powder

½ teaspoon salt

¼ teaspoon baking soda

½ cup confectioners sugar

1 Tablespoon orange juice

1 Tablespoon grated orange zest

1. Preheat the oven to 350°.
2. Spray a 15½ × 10½ × 1-inch baking pan with cooking spray.
3. Combine the butter and brown sugar in a large saucepan. Cook and stir constantly until the butter is melted.
4. Beat the applesauce, 1 teaspoon orange zest, egg, and vanilla into the saucepan mixture.
5. Sift the flour, baking powder, salt, and baking soda into a bowl. Combine.
6. Stir the dry ingredients into the saucepan ingredients.
7. Spread the batter into the greased pan.
8. Bake for 15 minutes.
9. While the brownies are baking, prepare the glaze by stirring together the confectioners sugar and orange juice until smooth.
10. Stir in the 1 Tablespoon orange zest until evenly distributed.
11. Remove the brownies from the oven and top with the glaze.
12. Let cool, and then cut into squares.

A moist brownie with a surprising flavor!

These brownies include nearly everything except the kitchen sink! And you don't have to stick with the ingredients in the recipe. Add what you like best—different nuts, Heath Bar bits, chunks of Oreo Cookies, marshmallows, pretzel pieces, small chunks of salted caramel, bits of Andes mints—whatever tempts you and those you're serving.

Blondies, Brunettes, and Redheads

Kitchen Sink Brownies

YVONNE MARTIN

Makes about 24 brownies

Prep Time: 15 minutes   *Baking Time: 30-35 minutes*

1½ cups semisweet chocolate chips

16 Tablespoons (2 sticks) butter

1½ cups sugar

1 teaspoon vanilla

4 eggs

1½ cups flour

½ teaspoon salt

¾ cup milk chocolate M&M's, *divided*

¼ cup milk chocolate chips

¼ cup white chocolate chips

¼ cup butterscotch, peanut butter, *or* cinnamon chips

½ cup chopped pecans, *optional*

1. Preheat the oven to 350°. Spray or grease a 9 × 13-inch baking pan.
2. Melt 1½ cups semisweet chips and butter in the microwave in 15-second intervals. Stir after each time. Continue until there are no lumps.
3. Mix in the sugar and vanilla.
4. In a separate bowl, beat the eggs well, and then stir them into the dough.
5. Add the flour and salt and beat well.
6. Mix ½ cup of the M&M's, all the 3 kinds of chips, and the pecans if you wish, into the batter. Pour into the baking pan.
7. Sprinkle the remaining M&M's over top.
8. Bake for about 20 minutes. Reduce the heat to 325°. Bake an additional 10 to 15 minutes or until the brownies test done in the center of the pan with a toothpick.
9. Allow to cool completely before cutting into squares.

Aunt Norma's Brownies

ELLEN GUTMAN CHENAUX

Makes 16 servings

Prep Time: 20-25 minutes ✿ *Baking Time: 18-25 minutes* ✿ *Cooling Time: 1 hour*

4 squares unsweetened chocolate

16 Tablespoons (2 sticks) butter

4 eggs

2 cups sugar

2 teaspoons vanilla

1½ cups flour

1 teaspoon baking powder

1 teaspoon salt

1 cup chopped walnuts

1 cup raisins

1. Preheat the oven to 350°. Grease a 9 × 13-inch baking pan, or two 8-inch square baking pans.
2. In a double boiler, melt the chocolate and butter over hot water, stirring frequently. Or melt the chocolate and butter slowly in the microwave, 15 seconds at a time, stirring after each time.
3. Scrape the chocolate-butter mixture into a bowl. Using a stand mixer (at medium speed), a hand mixer, or a wooden spoon and your hand, add the eggs, sugar, and vanilla. Blend until well mixed.
4. In a smaller bowl, mix together the flour, baking powder, and salt. Add these dry ingredients to the egg mixture, mixing until well blended. Stir in the nuts and raisins. Mix well.
5. Bake 18-25 minutes (the center will be soft). (Bake for 15-18 minutes if you're using the two square pans.) The timing is crucial with this recipe. If you like fudgy brownies, bake for the shortest amount of time. If you like them cakier, bake for the longer time.
6. Cool completely for at least an hour. Then cut into squares.

Variation: You can substitute dried cherries for the raisins. Two suggestions: 1.) If the cherries have sugar added, reduce the sugar in the recipe by 2 Tablespoons. 2.) You may want to soak the cherries in warm cherry liqueur or brandy for an extra-special experience.

Blondies, Brunettes, and Redheads

Raisins in brownies? You betcha! It's a real challenge to improve this brownie recipe, but a scoop of premium vanilla ice cream does take it to new heights.

Lemon Brownies

LYNNETTE SCOFIELD

Makes 12 squares

Prep Time: 15 minutes ❧ *Baking Time: 25 minutes* ❧ *Cooling Time: 1 hour*
Standing Time: 40 minutes

¾ cup flour

¾ cup sugar

¼ teaspoon salt

8 Tablespoons butter (1 stick),
softened to room temperature

2 large eggs

2 Tablespoons lemon zest

2 Tablespoons freshly
squeezed lemon juice

1 cup confectioners sugar

4 Tablespoons freshly
squeezed lemon juice

2 Tablespoons lemon zest

1. Preheat the oven to 350°. Grease an 8 × 8-inch baking dish with non-stick spray and set aside.
2. Beat together the flour, sugar, salt, and butter until well combined.
3. Add the eggs, 2 Tablespoons lemon zest, and 2 Tablespoons lemon juice. Beat until smooth and creamy, about 1 minute.
4. Pour into the prepared baking dish and bake for 25 minutes or until the edges are golden brown.
5. Allow to cool completely before glazing.
6. Prepare the glaze by sifting the confectioners sugar into a bowl. Stir in the 4 Tablespoons lemon juice and 2 Tablespoons zest.
7. Spread half of the glaze over the brownies and allow it to set, about 20 minutes.
8. When set, pour the remaining glaze over the brownies. Allow to set again before serving.
9. To serve, cut into 12 small squares.

A little cake, a little brownie. A lot of flavor!

It Takes
the Cake

Lemon Olive Oil Cake

LYNNETTE SCOFIELD

Makes 8 servings

Prep Time: 15 minutes ❧ *Baking Time: 30-35 minutes* ❧ *Cooling Time: 10 minutes*

1½ cups flour, plus
2 Tablespoons for
dusting the baking pan

¾ cup sugar

1 teaspoon baking soda

½ teaspoon salt

½ cup fresh lemon juice

⅓ cup olive oil

1 teaspoon grated
lemon zest

confectioners sugar
for dusting

1. Preheat the oven to 350°. Spray an 8-inch round baking pan with cooking spray, then dust with two tablespoons of flour, tapping out the excess.
2. Combine 1½ cups flour, sugar, baking soda, and salt into a good-sized mixer bowl.
3. Add the lemon juice, olive oil, and lemon zest. Using the mixer, mix on low speed until the ingredients are well combined.
4. Scrape the batter into the prepared pan with a spatula.
5. Bake for about 30-35 minutes or until a toothpick inserted into the center of the cake comes out clean and the sides begin to pull away from the side of the pan.
6. Let the cake cool for 10 minutes. Then invert the pan onto a plate, removing the cake. Allow the cake to cool completely.
7. Dust with confectioners sugar, cut into wedges, and serve.

This is the perfect cake for dessert with a glass of California wine, or in the morning as coffee cake with a hot beverage.

Easy Glazed Buttermilk Cake

KATHRYN WHITE

Makes 8-10 servings

Prep Time: 15 minutes 🌿 *Baking Time: 25 minutes*

1 cup flour

¾ cup sugar

½ teaspoon baking powder

½ teaspoon baking soda

½ teaspoon salt

1 large egg

⅓ cup buttermilk

1 teaspoon vanilla

4 Tablespoons (half a stick) butter, melted

8 Tablespoons (1 stick) butter

½ cup sugar

¼ cup buttermilk

1 teaspoon light corn syrup

½ teaspoon baking soda

½ teaspoon vanilla

1. Preheat the oven to 375°. Grease an 8 × 8-inch square baking pan.
2. In a small bowl combine the flour, ¾ cup sugar, baking powder, ½ teaspoon baking soda, and salt. Set aside.
3. In a medium bowl, whisk the egg, ⅓ cup buttermilk, and 1 teaspoon vanilla together until blended. Add the 4 Tablespoons butter and whisk to blend.
4. Add the flour mixture to the buttermilk mixture. Mix with a spoon until well combined.
5. Pour the batter into the prepared baking pan. Bake for 25 minutes or until a tester inserted into the center of the cake comes out clean.
6. While the cake is baking, prepare the glaze. Melt 8 Tablespoons butter in a small saucepan over medium heat.
7. Stir in ½ cup sugar, ¼ cup buttermilk, syrup, and ½ teaspoon baking soda. Bring to a boil and cook for 2 minutes, stirring frequently.
8. Remove from heat and stir in the vanilla.
9. Poke holes in the finished cake with a toothpick. Pour the hot glaze over the cake, distributing it evenly.
10. Cool the cake in the pan on a wire rack.
11. Slice and serve.

Orange Marmalade Cake

YVONNE MARTIN

Makes 10 servings

Prep Time: 20 minutes   *Baking Time: 25-30 minutes*

The marmalade topping makes this cake memorable.

16 Tablespoons (2 sticks) butter, softened to room temperature

2 cups sugar

3 eggs, *divided*

3 cups flour

1 Tablespoon baking powder

½ teaspoon salt

2 teaspoons grated orange zest

1 cup milk, *divided*

¼ cup orange juice

1 teaspoon vanilla extract

2 Tablespoons frozen orange juice concentrate

¼ cup orange juice

¼ cup sugar

1¼ cups orange marmalade

1. Preheat the oven to 350°. Grease and flour two 9-inch cake pans.
2. Cream the butter and gradually add the sugar. Add the eggs one at a time, beating well after each addition.
3. In a separate bowl, combine the flour, baking powder, salt, and orange zest.
4. Add ⅓ of this mixture to the butter mixture and then add half the milk.
5. Repeat. Beat in the remaining flour mixture, followed by ¼ cup orange juice and vanilla.
6. Pour the batter into the two prepared pans. Bake for 25 to 30 minutes or until the cakes are golden brown and spring back when touched.
7. Remove the cakes from the oven. Allow them to cool for 15 minutes. Then remove from their pans.
8. Place one cake upside down on a serving plate. (You may need to trim off part of the top so it sits flat.)
9. Make the glaze by heating the orange juice concentrate and ¼ cup orange juice in the microwave for 20 seconds.
10. Add the sugar and stir until dissolved.
11. Gently brush this syrup over the two cakes.
12. If the marmalade is stiff when you're ready to fill and top the cake, microwave it slightly to make it easier to spread. Spread half of the marmalade over the cake on the serving plate.
13. Place the other layer on top immediately. Spread the remaining marmalade over the top of the cake.

Mounds Cake

YVONNE MARTIN

Makes: 14 servings

Prep Time: 20 minutes *Baking Time: 1 hour*

2 eggs, separated

½ teaspoon almond extract

½ cup sugar

¼ cup flour

⅔ cup sweetened flaked coconut

2¾ cups flour

1 cup unsweetened cocoa powder

2 teaspoons baking powder

½ teaspoon salt

16 Tablespoons (2 sticks) butter, melted and cooled slightly

2 eggs

2 cups sugar

1 cup milk

½ cup water

1 teaspoon vanilla

½ teaspoon almond extract

confectioners sugar to garnish

1. Preheat the oven to 350°. Spray a Bundt or tube pan with non-stick cooking spray.
2. Make the filling first by separating the eggs and putting the whites in a mixer bowl. Save the yolks for the cake batter.
3. Add ½ teaspoon almond extract to the egg whites. Beat with a mixer at high speed.
4. Gradually beat in ½ cup of sugar and continue beating until soft peaks form.
5. Gently fold in ¼ cup of flour and the coconut. Set aside.
6. Make the cake batter by stirring together 2¾ cups flour, cocoa powder, baking powder, and salt. Set aside.
7. Put the melted butter and two eggs, plus the 2 reserved egg yolks, into a mixing bowl.
8. Beat at high speed, gradually beating in the 2 cups of sugar.
9. Beat in the milk, water, and vanilla.
10. Gradually beat in the flour and cocoa powder mixture.
11. Spread half of the cake batter in the prepared pan.
12. Spoon the coconut filling in a ring on top of the batter, making sure none of it touches the sides of the pan.

13. Carefully spoon the rest of the batter over the filling. Smooth the top.
14. Bake for about an hour or until the cake tests done when a toothpick or tester is inserted into its center.
15. Allow to cool before removing from the pan.
16. Dust with confectioners sugar before serving.

This cake gets its name from containing the two flavors in Mounds' candy bars—coconut and almond.

Prize-Winning Apple Cake

ELLEN GUTMAN CHENAUX

Serves: 10

Prep Time: 15 minutes ❧ *Baking Time: 55 minutes* ❧ *Cooling Time: 5-10 minutes*

I won first place with this cake at Lenox, Massachusetts' annual Apple Squeeze contest. Like most great recipes, this one has been handed from friend to friend, and it came to me from my college roommate. She got the recipe from her sister and when her sister's husband baked it for a contest, he, too, won first prize. Try it and you'll know why!

You will need to use a springform pan with a tube in the center for this cake. I bought a pan like this just for this cake, and it has been well used.

3-5 cooking apples,* peeled, cored and cut into 16ths**

8 Tablespoons (1 stick) unsalted butter, melted

1 cup sugar

2 eggs

2 cups flour

2 teaspoons baking powder

¼ teaspoon baking soda

¼ teaspoon salt

1 teaspoon vanilla

½ cup sour cream, *or* plain yogurt (not reduced fat)

cinnamon to taste

8 Tablespoons (1 stick) butter, melted

1 cup sugar

2 eggs

confectioners sugar

Rome, Cortland, Empire, or Granny Smith

**First cut the apple in half; then cut each half in halves; and then cut each quarter in half.*

1. Preheat your oven to 350°.
2. Grease the spring-form pan with a tube in the center.
3. Prepare the apples and set them aside.
4. Using an electric mixer, mix together 1 stick of melted butter, 1 cup sugar, and 2 eggs.
5. In a separate bowl, mix together the flour, baking powder, baking soda, and salt.
6. Add the mixed dry ingredients, vanilla, and sour cream (or yogurt) to the butter mixture. The batter will be somewhat stiff.
7. Scrape the batter into the well-greased pan.
8. Insert the apples with the cored side down, as close to each other as possible. Push the apples down into the batter.
9. Sprinkle liberally with the cinnamon.
10. Bake for 35 minutes. (The cake will not be done.)
11. While the cake is baking, make the topping by mixing 1 stick of melted butter, 1 cup sugar, and 2 eggs together.
12. After the first 35 minutes of baking, pour the topping over the hot cake. Bake for an additional 20 minutes.
13. Cool on a rack 5-10 minutes.
14. Carefully run a knife around the rim and remove the side of the pan. Flip the cake upside down on a platter and carefully remove the bottom of the pan. Flip the cake onto a serving plate. Cool completely.
15. Sprinkle with confectioners sugar before serving.

Almond Cake with Raspberry Coulis

YVONNE MARTIN

Makes 10-12 servings

Prep Time: 20 minutes ❧ *Baking Time: 45 minutes*

16 Tablespoons (2 sticks) butter, softened to room temperature

2 cups sugar

2 eggs, *divided*

2 cups flour

½ cup ground almonds

1½ teaspoons baking powder

¼ teaspoon salt

2 teaspoons almond extract

1 cup sour cream

¼ cup blanched sliced, *or* slivered, almonds

3 Tablespoons confectioners sugar

12-ounce bag frozen raspberries, thawed

¾ cup sugar

fresh mint leaves

1. Preheat the oven to 325°. Grease and flour a 9- or 10-inch round springform pan.
2. Cream the butter and gradually beat in the 2 cups sugar.
3. When well mixed, beat in the eggs, one at a time.
4. In a separate bowl, combine the flour, ground almonds, baking powder, and salt. Gently fold these dry ingredients into the butter mixture.
5. When well mixed, stir in the almond extract and sour cream. The batter will be very thick.
6. Spoon the batter into the prepared cake pan. Level the top and sprinkle sliced almonds evenly over the batter.
7. Bake for about 45 minutes or until a toothpick inserted into the center comes out clean.
8. Allow to cool. Remove from pan. Sieve confectioners sugar over top.
9. To make the coulis, combine the raspberries and ¾ cup sugar in a blender or food processor. Blend on low until combined.
10. To serve, slice the cake into 10 or 12 slices and place on plates. Spoon about 2 tablespoons of the raspberry sauce into a pool beside the cake. Garnish with fresh mint if available.

It Takes the Cake

This is a fairly dense and moist cake.
It looks very pretty on a plate.

Pound Cake with Macerated Strawberries

DANIELLE HANSCOM THODE

Makes 2 loaves, 8-10 slices each (One loaf can be frozen for a month for later use.)

Prep Time: 20 minutes ❧ *Baking Time: 60-70 minutes* ❧ *Cooling Time: 10 minutes*

4 cups flour

1 teaspoon baking powder

1 teaspoon salt

1 pound (4 sticks) unsalted butter, softened to room temperature

2 cups white sugar

8 large eggs, at room temperature, *divided*

2 teaspoons pure vanilla extract

finely grated zest and juice of one large lemon

1. Preheat oven to 325°. Spray two 4 × 12 × 3-inch baking (loaf) pans with non-stick cooking spray.
2. Sift together flour, baking powder, and salt in a large bowl. Set aside.
3. In the bowl of an electric mixer beat butter and sugar together until light and fluffy, about 6 minutes.
4. Add eggs one at a time, beating well after each addition. Mix in vanilla, lemon zest, and juice.
5. Gradually add the flour mixture, mixing gently until totally incorporated.
6. Distribute the batter evenly between the two pans and bake in the preheated oven for 1 hour to 1 hour and 10 minutes or until an inserted wooden toothpick comes out clean. Don't over-bake the loaves.
7. Cool 10 minutes before turning the cakes out onto a wire rack. Cool completely.
8. Cut into ½-inch-thick slices. Top each with fresh strawberries, peaches, or any fresh fruit in season.

This is a quintessential pound cake. We bake it in loaf pans, topping the slices with fresh strawberries, peaches, or any fresh fruit in season. We freeze leftover slices and use them at a later date for making trifles.

It Takes the Cake

Macerated Strawberries

DANIELLE HANSCOM THODE

Makes enough to serve with one pound cake loaf

Prep Time: 30 minutes

1 quart ripe but still firm strawberries

1 – 2 Tablespoons organic sugar

1 – 2 Tablespoons aged balsamic vinegar. Don't skimp on the quality!

mint leaves for garnish

1. Cut the strawberries into quarters into a small bowl.
2. Add 1 Tablespoon of sugar and one Tablespoon of balsamic vinegar. Let sit for 15–20 minutes and then taste. Add a little more sugar or vinegar if needed. Let sit a bit longer. You want the strawberries to get really juicy.
3. Spoon the strawberries, including the juice, over the pound cake slices, a scone, or vanilla ice cream. Garnish each serving with a mint leaf.

Mocha Cheesecake

ELLEN GUTMAN CHENAUX

Makes 10-12 servings

Prep Time: 45 minutes ❧ *Baking Time: 45-50 minutes* ❧ *Chilling Time: at least 3-4 hours*

1¼ cups graham cracker crumbs

4 Tablespoons (half a stick) unsalted butter, melted

¼ cup sugar

8 oz. semisweet baking chocolate, broken into chunks

¼ cup double-strength prepared espresso, cooled

2 Tablespoons heavy cream

24 oz. cream cheese, softened to room temperature

1 cup sugar

2 large eggs

1 cup sour cream

¼ cup rum, preferably dark

1 teaspoon vanilla

1 Tablespoon confectioners sugar

1 Tablespoon unsweetened cocoa powder

chocolate curls

1. Preheat the oven to 350°.
2. In a medium-sized bowl, thoroughly blend the graham cracker crumbs with the butter and ¼ cup sugar with your fingers or a fork. Firmly and smoothly press the mixture into the bottom of an ungreased 8- or 9-inch springform pan.
3. Prepare the filling by melting the chocolate over low heat or in a microwave at 15-20-second intervals, stirring after each time.
4. Add the espresso and stir in the heavy cream. Set mixture aside.
5. Place the cream cheese in the bowl of a stand mixer. Add the sugar and eggs. Start beating on low speed. Continue beating until the mixture is smooth and well-blended, increasing the speed carefully to prevent spattering.
6. Add the chocolate mixture, sour cream, rum, and vanilla. Beat slowly until well blended.
7. Pour and scrape the batter into the springform pan. Bang the pan on the counter a few times. Air bubbles will rise to the top. Use a toothpick or the end of a paring knife to puncture the air bubbles.

It Takes the Cake

8. Bake for 45 minutes, or until the edges are puffed. The center will remain a little soft, but it will firm up during cooling.
9. Let the cake cool on a wire rack for several hours. If you're making this a day ahead, cover the cake with plastic wrap and refrigerate.
10. Remove the sides of the pan. Garnish, if you wish, with a blend of confectioners sugar and cocoa powder. Finish with chocolate curls.

I love New York!
I also love New York cheesecake!

Lime Cheesecake

KATHRYN WHITE

Makes 10-12 servings

Prep Time: 30 minutes ❧ *Baking Time: 50 minutes*
Cooling Time: 3-4 hours ❧ *Chilling Time: 8 hours, or overnight*

1 cup thin coconut cookies, finely crushed

½ teaspoon cinnamon

¼ teaspoon freshly grated nutmeg

6 Tablespoons (¾ stick) butter, melted

1 teaspoon lime zest

24 ounces cream cheese, softened to room temperature

1 cup sugar

1 cup sour cream

1 teaspoon vanilla

⅓ cup lime juice

1 Tablespoon lime zest

⅛ teaspoon salt

3 large eggs, *divided*

fresh lime slices, *optional*

1. Preheat oven to 350°. Grease or spray a 9½ × 3-inch springform pan.
2. Combine the crushed cookies, cinnamon, nutmeg, melted butter, and 1 teaspoon lime zest in a medium bowl. Stir until the crushed cookies are evenly coated.
3. Press the mixture onto the bottom and about ½ inch up the sides of the springform pan. Set the pan aside.
4. Use a stand mixer to beat the cream cheese until smooth. This could take 5 minutes. Blend in the sugar and sour cream.
5. Blend in the vanilla, lime juice, 1 Tablespoon lime zest, and salt. Scrape down the bowl as necessary.
6. Add the eggs one at a time, beating each time until just blended.
7. Gently pour the filling over the crust, being careful not to disturb it.
8. Bake for 50 minutes or until the cake is just beginning to firm up in the middle.
9. Turn the oven off, open the oven door a few inches, and let the cheesecake cool thoroughly in the oven, about 3-4 hours.

It Takes the Cake

10. Remove the cake from the oven when it reaches room temperature. Cover and refrigerate overnight.
11. The cheesecake can be made a day or two before serving. Garnish with slices of lime and serve chilled.

Variation: Use gluten-free graham crackers for the crust instead of coconut cookies. Add ¼ cup of sugar to the crust mixture if you use graham crackers.

This is a delightful variation on a traditional cheesecake.

Tiffany's White Chocolate Raspberry Cheesecake

KRISTIE ROSSET

Makes 12 servings

Prep Time: 45 minutes ❧ *Baking Time: 90 minutes* ❧ *Cooling Time: 10-12 hours*

2 cups chocolate cookie crumbs

4 Tablespoons (half a stick) butter, melted

10-oz. package frozen raspberries

2 Tablespoons sugar

2 teaspoons, and 1 Tablespoon, cornstarch, *divided*

½ cup water

2 cups high quality white chocolate chips

½ cup half-and-half

1 teaspoon vanilla extract

3 8-oz. packages cream cheese, softened to room temperature

½ cup sugar

3 eggs at room temperature, *divided*

1. Preheat the oven to 325°. Place a shallow pan of hot water on the bottom rack of the oven.
2. Grease the sides of a 9-inch springform pan.
3. In a medium bowl, mix together the cookie crumbs and melted butter. Press the mixture into the bottom of the springform pan.
4. In a saucepan, combine the raspberries, 2 Tablespoons sugar, 2 teaspoons cornstarch, and water. Bring to boil and continue boiling for 5 minutes until the sauce is thick.
5. Strain the sauce through a mesh strainer to remove the seeds. Pour the sauce into a squeeze bottle or Ziploc bag.
6. In a metal bowl over a pan of simmering water, melt the white chocolate chips with half-and-half, stirring occasionally until smooth. Or use the chocolate melt setting on your microwave if trustworthy. When the mixture is melted and smooth, whisk in 1 Tablespoon cornstarch and vanilla.
7. In a large bowl, beat the cream cheese and ½ cup sugar until smooth. Scrape the bowl and beaters throughout the process.

8. Beat in the eggs one at a time at a low speed, scraping the bowl and beaters after each addition.

9. Gently fold the white chocolate mixture into the cream-cheese mixture. Pour the batter over the crust.

10. Use a squeeze bottle, or Ziploc bag with a tiny corner cut off, to squeeze the raspberry sauce over the surface of the batter in round "puddles." Use a butter knife or thin spreader to pull through each puddle of raspberry sauce from top to bottom, continuing from one puddle to another without lifting the knife out of the batter. This technique will magically transform each sauce puddle into a delicate heart shape.

11. Bake for 30 minutes. Reduce the temperature to 275°. Bake an additional 60 minutes.

12. Turn off the oven. Keep the oven door closed for 30 minutes.

13. Open the oven door. Let the cake cool in the oven for an additional 30 to 60 minutes.

14. Allow the cheesecake to come to room temperature before covering and placing in the refrigerator or freezer.

15. Chill or freeze overnight or longer (8-10 hours) before removing from pan and serving.

For years I had the joy of working with Tiffany Wilson, our inn's first intern who became our wedding coordinator, innkeeper, and friend. She was the queen of cheesecake and loved experimenting with different types and flavors. Together we led cooking schools, including the divine cheesecakes. This one is perfect for any occasion to celebrate love.

Raspberry Meringue Cake

DEBBIE MOSIMANN

Serves 10-12

Prep Time: 20 minutes ✂ *Cooling and Assembly Time: 40 minutes*
Baking Time: 30-35 minutes

4 large eggs

1 cup milk

1 Tablespoon vanilla

2½ cups cake flour

1¼ cups sugar

1 teaspoon salt

2½ teaspoons baking powder

12 Tablespoons (1½ sticks butter),
cut into 1-inch or smaller cubes,
at a cool room temperature

3 egg whites

½ teaspoon salt

¾ cup sugar

pinch of cream of tartar

1 teaspoon vanilla (add after
you remove from the heat)

1 cup whipping cream

2 Tablespoons confectioners sugar

orange liqueur, *optional*

1 pint fresh raspberries

1. Preheat the oven to 350°.
2. Grease and flour two 8-inch cake pans. Line the bottoms with parchment paper and spray the paper with non-stick cooking spray.
3. To make the yellow cake base, combine the 4 eggs, milk, and 1 Tablespoon vanilla in a medium-sized bowl.
4. In the bowl of a stand mixer, combine the flour, 1¼ cups sugar, salt, and baking powder.
5. Whisk the dry ingredients for 30 seconds to combine. With your mixer on low to medium speed, slowly add the pieces of butter, a few pieces at a time. Beat until the dry ingredients are moistened by the butter and look like crumbly coarse sand. Scrape the sides and bottom of the bowl to make sure there is no dry flour.
6. With the mixer on low speed, slowly add approximately half the egg/milk mixture to the dry ingredients, increasing to medium speed for 1½ minutes until the batter is thick and fluffy.
7. Scrape the bowl and add the remaining egg/milk mixture slowly, scraping the bowl and beating for 20 seconds after each addition.
8. Bake for 30-35 minutes, or until a toothpick inserted in the center comes out clean.
9. Let the cakes cool in the pans for 10 minutes and then turn them out. Cool completely.

It Takes the Cake

10. Meanwhile, make the meringue by whisking together the 3 egg whites, ½ teaspoon salt, ¾ cup sugar, and cream of tartar in a metal bowl.

11. Put two inches of water into a large saucepan that's big enough to suspend the metal bowl from its top edge. The metal bowl, when resting in the saucepan, should not touch the water. Bring the water to a boil, all the while whisking the mixture in the bowl.

12. Lower the heat to medium and continue whisking until all of the sugar is dissolved. If you have a candy thermometer, it should reach 175°. The mixture will feel hot to the touch.

13. Remove the bowl from the heat. Using the mixer, blend in the 1 teaspoon vanilla.

14. Using the whisk attachment, whisk the mixture on high until stiff peaks form. Set aside.

15. Make the filling by whipping the cream until it's stiff, incorporating the confectioners sugar toward the end of the whipping process.

16. To assemble the cake, place one layer on a serving plate. Drizzle with orange liqueur if you like.

17. Spread all the whipped cream filling on top of this layer. Then distribute all the raspberries over top.

18. Place the second layer of cake on top of the raspberries. Sprinkle with orange liqueur if you like.

19. Spread all the meringue on top, making attractive peaks as you go. With a blow torch brown the meringue gently.

20. Refrigerate until serving.

This is a dessert you can make when
you want to impress. It looks and tastes
as good as anything from a fancy
bakery. But it's really easy to make
and garnish, even for those of us with no
decorating skill whatsoever. This is a rich
cake, so smaller servings are better.

It Takes the Cake

Strawberry Truffle Cake

YVONNE MARTIN

Serves 10-12

Prep Time: 30 minutes ❧ *Baking Time: 35-40 minutes*
Chilling Time: at least 2 hours

8 Tablespoons (1 stick) butter, softened to room temperature

1 cup sugar

3 eggs

1 cup chocolate syrup

1 cup flour

1 teaspoon baking powder

8 oz. semisweet baking chocolate

8 oz. package cream cheese, softened to room temperature

¼ cup confectioners sugar

½ cup strawberry preserves

¼ cup white, *or* semisweet, chocolate

1 teaspoon butter

1. Spray a 9-inch round baking pan with non-stick spray. Line the bottom with parchment or wax paper and spray again.
2. To make the brownie base, cream the 8 Tablespoons butter and the 1 cup sugar together with a mixer.
3. Beat in the eggs. Beat in the chocolate syrup.
4. Gradually add the flour and baking powder and beat well.
5. Pour into the prepared pan. Bake at 350° for about 35 to 40 minutes, or until the top springs back when touched.
6. Allow to cool fully in the pan. Then turn upside down onto a cutting board and remove the parchment from the bottom of the cake. Return the brownie base to the pan.
7. To make the truffle layer, melt the baking chocolate in a microwave or over a double boiler.
8. Using a mixer, beat the cream cheese and confectioners sugar together.
9. Mix in the preserves and melted chocolate. Beat until smooth.
10. Spread evenly over the baked and cooled brownie base in its pan. Refrigerate for at least an hour.
11. To make the garnish, melt the white or semisweet chocolate and 1 teaspoon butter together in a microwave. Stir, then drizzle over top of the cake.
12. Refrigerate until ready to serve. Cut into 10 or 12 wedges.

Cranberry Orange Angel Food Cake

DANIELLE HANSCOM THODE

Makes 10-12 servings

Prep Time: 30 minutes ❧ *Baking Time: 30-35 minutes* ❧ *Cooling Time: 1-2 hours*

Perfect for the holiday season!

1½ cups egg whites (about 1 dozen egg whites), at room temperature

1¼ tsp. cream of tartar

½ tsp. salt

1½ cups sugar, *divided*

1 cup sifted unbleached flour

⅛ cup cornstarch

½ tsp. pure vanilla extract

½ tsp. pure orange extract

zest of one orange

1 cup chopped fresh cranberries

confectioners sugar

1. Preheat the oven to 375°.
2. Whip the egg whites in the bowl of a stand mixer, using the whisk attachment, until foamy. Whip in the cream of tartar and salt. Keep whipping until soft peaks form.
3. With the mixer running, gradually add 1 cup of sugar to the egg whites. Continue whipping until stiff peaks form and the sugar has dissolved. This will take about another 45 seconds.
4. In a separate bowl, sift the remaining ½ cup sugar with the flour and cornstarch 3 times. *Carefully* fold the flour into the egg whites.
5. When the flour is nearly blended into the whipped whites, gently add the vanilla and orange extracts, orange zest, and chopped cranberries, folding until the berries are evenly distributed. Don't over-mix.
6. Carefully spoon the batter into an ungreased angel food cake pan.
7. Bake for 30 to 35 minutes until the cake is light brown on top.
8. Cool the cake in the pan by putting it upside down on your counter if your pan has "feet." If it doesn't, turn the pan upside down on the neck of a bottle until the cake cools to room temperature.
9. Run a long, sharp knife blade between the cake and the sides of the pan and loosen the cake out onto a plate.
10. Sprinkle with confectioners sugar before cutting into slices with a serrated knife.

Waldorf Astoria Carrot Cake

ELLEN GUTMAN CHENAUX

Makes 12 servings

Prep Time: 20 minutes ❧ *Baking Time: 50-60 minutes*

2 cups sugar

1½ cups canola oil

2 teaspoons baking soda

2 cups flour

1 teaspoon cinnamon

1 teaspoon salt

4 eggs

3 cups finely grated carrots
(about 8 good-sized carrots)

½ cup chopped walnuts

8 ounces cream cheese,
softened to room temperature

4 Tablespoons (half a stick) butter,
softened to room temperature

1 pound confectioners sugar

2 teaspoons rum, *or* rum flavoring

1 Tablespoon milk

1. Preheat the oven to 350°.
2. Grease a 9 × 13-inch baking pan.
3. Stir the sugar and oil together in a large bowl.
4. In a medium bowl, mix the baking soda, flour, cinnamon, and salt together. Add to the sugar/oil mixture.
5. Add the eggs. Add the carrots and nuts. Mix well.
6. Pour into the greased pan. Bake for 50-60 minutes, or until a tester inserted into the center of the cake comes out clean. Cool.
7. To make the frosting, cream together the cream cheese, butter, confectioners sugar, and rum, using the 1 Tablespoon milk to soften.
8. Spread the frosting on the cooled cake.

Culinary legend has it that the ever-popular carrot cake was born at the famed New York hotel, The Waldorf Astoria. Whatever its origins, I guarantee you will fall in love with this one.

How Sweet It Is

Chocolate Peanut Butter Candy Squares
(aka peanut butter cups)

KRISTIE ROSSET

Makes 40 squares

Prep Time: 20 minutes ✿ *Chilling Time: 1-3 hours*

16 Tablespoons (2 sticks) butter

1 cup crunchy, *or* creamy, peanut butter

1¾ cups graham cracker crumbs

2 cups confectioners sugar

12-oz. package milk chocolate chips

1 teaspoon shortening, *optional*

1. Spray a 9 × 13-inch baking pan with non-stick spray.
2. Place the butter in a medium-sized microwave-safe bowl. Melt the butter, checking frequently to stir until it's completely melted.
3. Add peanut butter, graham cracker crumbs, and confectioners sugar to the butter. Stir until well mixed.
4. Press the mixture into the bottom of the prepared pan. Smooth.
5. Melt the chocolate chips with shortening, if you wish, in the microwave, stirring every 30 seconds until melted. Do not overcook.
6. Spread the chocolate evenly over the base.
7. Chill for one or more hours.
8. Cut into squares to serve.

Hint: Allow the candy to rest at room temperature for a few minutes prior to cutting. Sometimes the chocolate breaks when cutting, but the taste is not impacted. It's all good.

I love Reese's Peanut Butter Cups, as do my son-in-law and grandson. I cannot give the candy to trick-or-treaters, because I'll eat the entire bag before they show up. This recipe is a real treat, and in our home I make it only during the holidays.

How Sweet It Is

Traditional Chocolate Fudge
(by a non-traditional method)

KRISTIE ROSSET

Makes 20 pieces

Prep Time: 15 minutes   Chilling Time: 1-2 hours

8 Tablespoons (1 stick) butter, softened to room temperature

1 pound (4 cups) confectioners sugar

⅓–½ cup unsweetened cocoa powder (I prefer ⅓ cup)

¼ cup milk

pinch of salt

1 teaspoon vanilla

½ cup chopped pecans, *or* walnuts

1. Place the butter, confectioners sugar, cocoa powder, milk, and salt in a medium-sized glass mixing bowl. Microwave on high for 2 minutes.
2. Stir with a hand mixer, or by hand with a wooden spoon, until smooth and all ingredients are evenly incorporated.
3. Stir in the vanilla and nuts until well mixed.
4. Line an 8 × 8-inch baking pan with wax paper. Pour the fudge into the pan.
5. Chill until firm, about 1-2 hours. Cut into squares and enjoy.

For decades, my sister has made this delicious fudge that is beloved by our extended family. It's super- easy to make.

This is the perfect "do it your way" recipe. Like nuts? Add whatever you'd like. Holiday? Add crushed peppermint candies. Have leftover cookies? Why not? This is yours to design.

How Sweet It Is

White Chocolate Bark

LYNNETTE SCOFIELD

12 servings

Prep Time: 10 minutes ❧ *Microwave Time: 1-2 minutes* ❧ *Chilling Time: 2 hours*

2 cups white chocolate chips

4 drops vegetable oil

¾ cup chopped dried cranberries, *or* chopped apricots, *or* other ingredients that sound good to you

1. Put the white chocolate chips in a microwave-safe bowl.
2. Microwave on level 3, or 30% power, in 30-second increments. Stir after each 30 seconds. Continue to microwave until the chocolate is smooth and no chip shapes are visible.
3. Add drops of vegetable oil to make a smooth and satiny mixture.
4. Spray a parchment-lined jelly roll pan with non-stick cooking spray. Spread the chocolate out on the parchment.
5. Scatter dried fruits, nuts, or other ingredients that you enjoy over top.
6. Place in the refrigerator until chilled thoroughly, about two hours.
7. Remove from refrigerator and break into shards. This doesn't have to be neat!

Note: This does not keep more than two days!

Homemade Marshmallows

LYNNETTE SCOFIELD

Yield: One pound and 10 ounces of goodness

Prep Time: 30 minutes ❧ *Cooking Time: 20 minutes* ❧ *Standing Time: 8-12 hours*

We LOVED being able to offer homemade marshmallows to our guests at the Inn. Yes, they loved them in homemade hot chocolate, but mainly they were fascinated that we actually made them!

vegetable shortening
(Crisco is best) for
preparing the pan

1 cup cold water,
divided

3 Tablespoons
(3 envelopes)
unflavored gelatin

2 cups sugar

¾ cup light corn syrup

¼ teaspoon salt

1½ teaspoons vanilla

confectioner's
sugar for coating

1. Line a 9 × 13-inch baking pan thoroughly with foil. Coat the foil with vegetable shortening. Set the pan aside.
2. Place ½ cup of cold water in the large bowl of a stand mixer and sprinkle all the gelatin over the surface of the water. Set aside.
3. Place the sugar, corn syrup, salt, and the remaining ½ cup water in a heavy saucepan over low heat.
4. Stir until the sugar dissolves and the mixture comes to a boil.
5. Turn off the heat. Cover the saucepan, and let the mixture stand for three minutes.
6. Uncover and raise the heat to high.
7. Using a candy thermometer, let the syrup boil (do not stir!) until the temperature reaches 240°.
8. Remove from the heat.
9. Turn the stand mixer on to medium speed.
10. Pour the syrup into the gelatin mixture.
11. Increase the speed to high. Beat for 15 minutes until it looks like beautiful marshmallows. Scrape the bowl occasionally.
12. Just before you are done beating, add the vanilla.
13. Pour this beautiful mixture into the prepared pan. Smooth the top.
14. Let stand uncovered for 8 to 12 hours.
15. Sift the confectioners sugar onto a cutting board larger than your pan.
16. Turn the marshmallows over onto the sugar, removing the pan and the foil.
17. Use a pizza cutter to cut into pieces the size you want.
18. Roll all sides of the marshmallows in the confectioners sugar.
19. Store in a covered container or secure plastic bag.

These make a colorful and pretty addition to
a holiday tray of sweet treats.

How Sweet It Is

Coconut Strawberries

YVONNE MARTIN

Makes about 60 strawberries

Prep Time: 30 minutes *Chilling Time: 30 minutes*

14-oz. can sweetened
condensed milk

3 3-oz. packages strawberry
gelatin, *divided*

4 cups shredded
coconut, *divided*

½ cup green frosting

1. Pour the condensed milk into a good-sized bowl. Mix in two packages of gelatin and 2 cups of coconut.
2. Gradually mix in more coconut until mixture is firm and dry enough to mold into shapes.
3. Empty the third package of gelatin into a small bowl.
4. Break off tablespoon-size pieces of the coconut mixture and form into strawberry shapes. Roll each strawberry in the dry gelatin to coat.
5. Place on a cookie sheet lined with waxed paper or parchment. Using a small icing bag and tip, pipe green frosting leaves at the top of each strawberry.
6. Refrigerate for 30 minutes before serving. Store in an airtight container in the fridge until needed.

Swedish Pecans

JOYCE SCHULTE

Makes 1 pound coated nuts

Prep Time: 5 minutes ✂ *Baking Time: 60 minutes*

1 pound pecan halves

8 Tablespoons
(1 stick) butter

2 egg whites

dash salt

1 cup sugar

1 teaspoon vanilla

1. Spread nuts on a rimmed baking sheet.
2. Bake at 250° for 15 minutes.
3. Remove nuts from oven and from the baking sheet. (Don't turn the oven off.) Cool nuts on wax paper.
4. Slice butter and scatter over baking sheet pan. Place in oven to melt.
5. In a good-sized bowl, mix the egg whites, salt, sugar, and vanilla together.
6. Fold the nuts into the meringue until they're all covered.
7. Spoon the nut mixture on to the pan of melted butter.
8. Bake at 275° for 15 minutes.
9. Turn over with a spatula. Bake another 30 minutes turning every 10 minutes until golden brown.
10. Allow to cool before breaking up and either serving or storing.

This is an old recipe of my mother's. These nuts always showed up at our house around holiday time. I started making them for Christmas presents when I was in college and still find them a great gift or a great treat to take to work and share. But hey, why wait for a holiday? Buttery, sugary nuts are welcome anytime.

How Sweet It Is

Spiced Pecans

KRISTIE ROSSET

Makes 2 cups

Prep Time: 10 minutes ✻ *Baking Time: 30 minutes*

2 Tablespoons (¼ stick) butter, melted

1 Tablespoon Worcestershire sauce

⅛ teaspoon ground cayenne pepper (more or less depending upon how much heat you and your guests like)

¼ teaspoon salt

¼ teaspoon garlic powder

1 Tablespoon chili powder

2 cups pecan halves

1. Preheat oven to 300°.
2. Mix together butter, Worcestershire sauce, and seasonings in a medium bowl. Stir until thoroughly mixed.
3. Add the pecans and stir gently.
4. Spread pecans on a rimmed baking sheet. Bake for 30 minutes, stirring every 10 minutes.

A nice counterpoint to sweet pecans. Adjust the cayenne pepper or chili powder to your preferred level of spicy/hot. Some like it with up to ¼ teaspoon cayenne; I prefer ⅛ teaspoon. This provides some kick without the pain. Or you can leave out the cayenne completely if you choose.

Evil Toffee

YVONNE MARTIN

Yield depends on your willpower. Should be about 12 servings.

Prep Time: 15 minutes ❧ *Baking Time: 5 minutes* ❧ *Chilling Time: 60 minutes*

about 24 saltine crackers,
enough to cover the bottom
of the baking pan

16 Tablespoons (2 sticks)
butter (no substitute)

1 cup brown sugar

1½ cups chocolate chips

1. Preheat oven to 350°.
2. Line a 9 × 13-inch baking pan with foil. Grease it with butter or non-stick spray.
3. Lay the crackers in a single layer on the pan, salt side down.
4. Melt butter in a medium saucepan.
5. Stir in brown sugar and bring to a boil over medium heat. Boil for 3 minutes. Pour over crackers.
6. Put in oven for 5 minutes.
7. Remove and sprinkle the chocolate chips. Let the chips melt, and then spread evenly over toffee.
8. Refrigerate for about an hour before breaking into uneven pieces.

This popular confection earned its name because
it lurks in your refrigerator, calling out
its siren song, tempting everyone to eat it.

Cobblers, Crumbles, Crisps

A summer treat at our inn! Tapioca is wonderful for thickening fruit cobblers, pies, and crisps because it can be cooked for a prolonged time and doesn't break down when acid, such as lemon juice, is added. And it gives the filling a nice sheen.

Cobblers, Crumbles, Crisps

Peach Cobbler

DANIELLE HANSCOM THODE

Serves 6-8

Prep Time: 40 minutes *Baking time: 45-55 minutes*

8 cups peaches, peeled and cut into ¼-inch slices

2 Tablespoons freshly squeezed lemon juice

½ cup sugar

½ cup brown sugar

3 Tablespoons minute tapioca

1 teaspoon vanilla

¼ teaspoon freshly grated nutmeg

1½ cups flour

2 teaspoons baking powder

½ teaspoon freshly grated nutmeg

2 Tablespoons sugar

¼ teaspoon salt

6 Tablespoons (¾ stick) unsalted butter, cold and cubed

¾ cup whole milk, mixed with 1 teaspoon vanilla extract

1 Tablespoon sugar for sprinkling before baking

1. Preheat the oven to 350°. Butter a 9 or 10-inch (2½-quart) oval, ovenproof dish.
2. In a large bowl mix the peaches with lemon juice, ½ cup sugar, ½ cup brown sugar, tapioca, 1 teaspoon vanilla, and ¼ teaspoon grated nutmeg.
3. Pour into the prepared dish. Set aside for at least 10 minutes while preparing the topping.
4. Mix the flour, baking powder, ½ teaspoon grated nutmeg, 2 Tablespoons sugar, and salt in the mixing bowl of a food processor.
5. Add the cold, cubed butter. Pulse until the mixture resembles coarse oatmeal.
6. Add the milk/vanilla mixture. Pulse until just blended. Do not over-mix.
7. Spoon the topping over the peach mixture. Sprinkle with 1 Tablespoon sugar.
8. Bake 45 to 55 minutes until the top is golden and the peaches are bubbly. Check after 30 minutes. Cover with a piece of foil if the top browns too quickly.

Peach Blueberry Crumble

ELLEN GUTMAN CHENAUX

Makes 6-8 servings

Prep Time: 10 minutes ✿ *Baking Time: 25-45 minutes, depending on the dish(es) you use*

½ cup brown sugar

½ cup flour

½ cup dry quick, *or* old-fashioned, oats

5 Tablespoons butter, softened to room temperature

3 large peaches, sliced (if fresh, leave the peels on)

½ cup fresh blueberries

¼ cup honey

juice of half a lemon

freshly grated nutmeg

1. Preheat the oven to 375°. Grease an 8-inch-square, or 6-cup deep baking dish, or 6-8 individual ramekins.
2. Make the topping by combining the brown sugar, flour, dry oats, and butter until well mixed. Set aside.
3. Place the peaches and blueberries in the greased baking dish(es). Drizzle with honey and the lemon juice.
4. Spoon the topping over the fruit mixture.
5. Grate the nutmeg over the crumble.
6. Bake for 40-45 minutes for the 8-inch baking dish; 25-30 minutes for the individual dishes or until the fruit is tender.
7. Serve warm. It's even better with a scoop of ice cream.

Variations

The combinations are endless. Use two peaches and two nectarines for Peach Nectarine Crumble.

Add a plum or two. In winter, use 3-4 apples and ½ cup raisins instead of the peaches and blueberries. Or 2 pears and 2 apples plus ½ cup cranberries for Pear Cranapple Crumble. Let your imagination go!

Bumbleberry Crisp

YVONNE MARTIN

Makes 8 to 12 servings

Prep Time: 15 minutes ✻ *Baking Time: 40-45 minutes*

5 cups rhubarb, *or* apples, cut into ½" pieces

1 cup sliced strawberries

1 cup blueberries

1 cup raspberries

1½ cups sugar

¼ cup flour

1 cup dry quick, *or* old-fashioned rolled, oats

1½ cups brown sugar

2 cups flour

16 Tablespoons (2 sticks) butter

ice cream, *or* whipped cream

1. Preheat the oven to 375°. Spray a 9 × 13-inch baking dish with non-stick cooking spray.
2. In a good-sized bowl, combine the rhubarb, strawberries, blueberries, and raspberries with the sugar and ¼ cup flour. Spread in the prepared dish.
3. Using a good-sized bowl, prepare the topping by mixing the dry oats, brown sugar, and 2 cups flour together.
4. Melt the butter in a large pot. Remove it from the heat and mix in the dry ingredients until crumbly.
5. Spread the crumbs evenly over the fruit mixture. Do NOT press down.
6. Bake at 375° for approximately 30 minutes.
7. Turn the oven down to 350° and continue baking for about 10 more minutes or until the fruit tests soft when pierced with a fork. This will take longer if you started out with frozen fruit.
8. Serve warm or cold with ice cream or whipped cream.

Note: Any or all of the fruit in the recipe can be fresh or frozen. If using all frozen fruit, allow about an extra 10 minutes of baking time.

This is one of our inn's signature desserts. We jokingly tell our guests that bumbleberries are unique to our area and that we pick them in the woods behind the inn.

You can substitute your own favorite berry or fruit for the cherries in this recipe. It's also wonderful made with blackberries, blueberries, peaches, apples, or raspberries.

Cobblers, Crumbles, Crisps

Cherry Crumble

YVONNE MARTIN

Makes 8-10 servings

Prep Time: 15 minutes ✻ *Baking Time: 30-40 minutes*

5 cups pitted cherries,
fresh *or* frozen

1 cup sugar

¼ cup cornstarch

1 teaspoon vanilla extract

½ teaspoon almond extract

½ teaspoon salt

2 cups flour

1½ cups brown sugar,
lightly packed

1 cup dry quick oats

16 Tablespoons
(2 sticks) butter

1. Preheat the oven to 350°. Grease a 9 × 13-inch baking dish, or 8 to 10 individual ramekins.
2. Combine the cherries, sugar, cornstarch, vanilla, almond extract, and salt. Spoon into the prepared baking dish(es).
3. Make the crumble topping by mixing the flour, brown sugar, and oats together in a good-sized bowl.
4. Melt the butter and mix into the flour mixture with a fork. Mixture should be crumbly.
5. Sprinkle the topping over the fruit.
6. Bake for about 40 minutes for a 9 × 13-inch dish, or 30 minutes for the ramekins. When done the crumble topping should be golden brown with the fruit juice bubbling up at the edges.

This cobbler is my go-to recipe loved by all. The fruit varies with the season, from peaches or blackberries, or my favorite—rhubarb and strawberries. Make this in June when both are fresh and in season. Use salted butter—it adds that something extra to the crust.

Cobblers, Crumbles, Crisps

Topsy-Turvy Strawberry Rhubarb Cobbler

DEBBIE MOSIMANN

Serves 8-10

Prep Time: 10 minutes ❧ *Baking Time: 30-35 minutes*

8 Tablespoons (1 stick) salted butter

1 quart strawberries, hulled and sliced

4 stalks rhubarb, trimmed and sliced into ¼-inch slices

2 cups flour

1¼ cups sugar

1 Tablespoon baking powder

1¾ cups milk

1. Preheat oven to 350°.
2. Cut up the butter and place the chunks in the bottom of a 9 × 13-inch baking pan. Or use 2 pie plates, dividing the butter between them. Put in the preheated oven to melt the butter for 5-10 minutes. Do not allow the butter to brown.
3. Prepare the fruit so it's ready when you pour the batter. Set it aside.
4. Mix the flour, sugar, and baking powder in a good-sized bowl. Combine with a whisk. Then whisk in the milk. The batter should be somewhat thin.
5. Remove the pan(s) with the butter from the oven. Pour the batter over the hot butter. It will start to puff around the edges.
6. Distribute the strawberries and rhubarb evenly over the batter. Return the filled pan(s) to the oven. Bake 30-35 minutes until the edges are browned and a toothpick inserted into the middle comes out clean.

Vegan Apple Crisp

DANIELLE HANSCOM THODE

Makes 6 servings

Prep Time: 20 minutes ❧ *Baking Time: 45 minutes* ❧ *Cooling Time: 15 minutes*

2 cups dry old-fashioned oats, *divided*

½ cup light brown sugar

¼ teaspoon fine sea salt

6 Tablespoons coconut oil, melted

2 Tablespoons fresh lemon juice

zest of one lemon

2 pounds (4-5) apples* peeled, cored and cut into ½ inch chunks

1 lemon, zest and juice

¼ cup light brown sugar

1 teaspoon ground ginger

* Granny Smith, Golden and/ or Gala. I prefer a mixture of different apples for the texture and flavor.

1. Preheat the oven to 375°. Grease an 8-inch square glass baking dish with a small amount of coconut oil.
2. To make the crumble, pulse 1½ cup oats in a food processor until coarsely chopped.
3. Place into a large bowl and add the other ½ cup oats, light brown sugar, salt, coconut oil, lemon juice, and zest. Stir with a fork until combined. Set aside.
4. To make the filling, toss together the apples, lemon zest and juice, light brown sugar, and ginger in a good-sized bowl. Transfer to the prepared baking dish.
5. Top with the oatmeal crumble. Cover with aluminum foil and bake 30 minutes.
6. Remove the foil and continue baking until the apples are tender and the topping is golden, about 15 minutes.
7. Remove from the oven. Let cool 15 minutes before serving.

This can easily be made into a gluten-free dessert by using gluten-free rolled oats.

Hi There, Cookie!

Flourless Monster Cookies

KRISTIE ROSSET

Makes 6-7 dozen cookies

Prep Time: 30 minutes *Baking Time: 12-15 minutes, per baking sheet*

16 Tablespoons (2 sticks)
butter, softened to
room temperature

2 cups sugar

2¼ cups packed dark
brown sugar

3 cups peanut butter,
chunky *or* creamy

6 eggs, *divided*

1 Tablespoon white corn syrup

½ Tablespoon vanilla extract

4 teaspoons baking soda

8 cups dry rolled oats

1½ cups plain M&M's

1½ cups semisweet chocolate
chips, *or* butterscotch chips

*Note: If your stand mixer is
small, consider making half
a batch at a time.*

1. Preheat the oven to 350°. Line each baking sheet with parchment paper.
2. In the bowl of a large stand mixer, cream together the butter and sugars until smooth. Add the peanut butter and beat until smooth.
3. Add the eggs, one at a time, beating after each addition to incorporate well.
4. Stir in the syrup, vanilla, and baking soda until well mixed.
5. Add the rolled oats in two batches, mixing thoroughly to incorporate.
6. Remove the bowl from the mixer. Stir in the candies and chips.
7. Drop in large spoonfuls on to the parchment-lined baking sheets. The cookies need room to grow, so don't place any more than 12 cookies on a baking sheet.
8. Bake 12-15 minutes until done. Cool for a couple of minutes on the baking sheet, then remove to finish cooling on wire racks.

Note: Although these cookies are flourless and may be tolerated by some gluten-free diets, they are not gluten-free unless the rolled oats are identified as gluten-free and processed in a gluten-free facility. If you use regular oats, celiac patients and others highly sensitive to gluten should not consume them.

Hi There, Cookie!

Coconut Macaroons

DANIELLE HANSCOM THODE

Makes about 3 dozen macaroons

Prep Time: 20 minutes ❧ *Chilling Time: 60 minutes*
Baking time: 10-12 minutes, per baking sheet

5⅓ Tablespoons butter,
softened to room temperature

3 oz. cream cheese, softened
to room temperature

¾ cup sugar

1 large egg yolk

2 teaspoons pure
almond extract

2 teaspoons milk

1¼ cups flour

2 teaspoons baking powder

½ teaspoon fine sea salt

4 cups flaked, sweet
coconut, *divided*

1. Preheat the oven to 325°. Line two baking sheets with parchment paper or silicone liners.
2. Cream the butter, cream cheese, and sugar in a large mixer bowl until light and fluffy.
3. Add the egg yolk, almond extract, and milk. Beat well.
4. In a medium-sized bowl, combine the flour, baking powder, and salt. Gradually fold the mixture into the creamed mixture.
5. Stir in 3 cups of coconut. Cover tightly and chill for one hour until firm.
6. Shape dough into 1½ inch balls (we use a small ice cream scoop to do this) and roll in remaining 1 cup of coconut flakes.
7. Place on the lined baking sheet 2 inches apart.
8. Bake 10 to 12 minutes, until barely golden.
9. Remove from oven and cool 5 minutes on the baking sheets before transferring cookies to a cooling rack. When completely cooled, store in an airtight container.

This is the perfect soft, scrumptious cookie for the coconut lover.

This cookie comes with a warning: 24 is not nearly enough and
you MUST be sure you have a quart of ice-cold milk on hand.
One thing is for sure... these are FABULOUS!

Hi There, Cookie!

Double Chocolate Chip Cookies with Sea Salt

LYNNETTE SCOFIELD

Makes 24 cookies

Prep Time: 10 minutes ❧ *Baking Time: 9-12 minutes, per baking sheet*

½ cup sugar

½ cup brown sugar

8 Tablespoons (1 stick) unsalted butter, melted

1 egg

1 teaspoon vanilla

1¼ cups flour

¼ cup unsweetened cocoa powder (a good place to splurge)

½ teaspoon baking soda

½ teaspoon salt

¾ cup chocolate chips (another good place to splurge)

1 Tablespoon sea salt (for the tops of the cookies)

1. Preheat the oven to 375°. Line two baking sheets with parchment paper.
2. In the large bowl of a stand mixer, combine the sugars and melted butter until well mixed. Remember to scrape down the bowl.
3. Add the egg and vanilla. Beat for about 30 seconds until well blended.
4. Sift the flour, cocoa powder, baking soda, and salt (but not the sea salt) together.
5. Add the dry to the wet ingredients, blending well.
6. Add the chocolate chips, stirring until well mixed.
7. In your hand, form the dough into small balls and place on the parchment, 2 inches apart.
8. Flatten the balls with palm of your hand or the bottom of a glass.
9. Sprinkle lightly with sea salt.
10. Bake 9-12 minutes.
11. Try to restrain yourself and wait until they cool.

Chocolate Crinkles

KATHRYN WHITE

Makes 3 dozen cookies

Prep Time: 15 minutes ✢ *Chilling Time: 1 hour*
Baking Time: 12 minutes, per baking sheet

When is it not a good time for chocolate? Adding espresso powder
to the dough adds punch and boosts the chocolate flavor.

1 cup flour

½ cup unsweetened
cocoa powder

1 teaspoon baking
powder

½ teaspoon salt

6 Tablespoons (¾ stick)
butter, cut into pieces

4 ounces unsweetened
chocolate, chopped

1¼ cups sugar

2 large eggs

2 teaspoons instant
espresso powder

1 teaspoon vanilla extract

½ cup confectioners
sugar

1. Preheat the oven to 325°. Line baking sheets with parchment paper or a silicone baking mat.
2. Whisk the flour, cocoa powder, baking powder, and salt together in a bowl.
3. Combine the butter and chocolate in a microwave-safe bowl. Melt the butter and chocolate in the microwave in 30-second increments. Stir after each increment until both are melted. You can also melt the butter and chocolate in a small saucepan on the stove over low heat.
4. Blend the sugar, eggs, espresso powder, and vanilla together in a large bowl. Add the melted chocolate to the egg mixture and blend.
5. Gradually add the flour mixture to the chocolate mixture, stirring to combine.
6. Cover the bowl and refrigerate the dough until firm, about an hour.
7. Remove the dough from the refrigerator. Shape into balls about an inch in diameter.
8. Put the confectioners sugar in a shallow bowl or saucer. Drop the balls into the confectioners sugar and roll to coat evenly.
9. Place the balls on the prepared cookie sheets, 2 inches apart and bake until the dough is puffy and cracked on top, about 12 minutes.
10. Remove the sheet from the oven and let cool 2 to 3 minutes before moving the cookies to a wire rack to finish cooling.
11. Store at room temperature in a covered container.

Chocolate Chip Coconut Toffee Cookies

(with Gluten-Free Option)

KATHRYN WHITE

Makes 4 dozen cookies

Prep Time: 15 minutes ❧ *Baking Time: 12-15 minutes, per baking sheet*

1½ cups flour

½ teaspoon baking powder

½ teaspoon baking soda

½ teaspoon salt

8 Tablespoons (1 stick) butter, softened to room temperature

½ cup sugar

½ cup packed dark brown sugar

1 large egg

½ teaspoon vanilla extract

1 cup semisweet chocolate chips

1 cup shredded unsweetened coconut

1 cup toffee bits

1. Preheat the oven to 325°.
2. Line a cookie sheet with a silicone mat or parchment paper.
3. Sift the flour, baking powder, baking soda, and salt together in a small bowl. Set aside.
4. In a large bowl, cream the butter until pale yellow and fluffy. Add both sugars and continue beating until the mixture is smooth. Add the egg and vanilla until blended. Be sure to scrape the sides of the bowl as needed.
5. Add the flour mixture and mix on low speed until just blended. Stir in the chocolate chips, coconut, and toffee bits until blended.
6. Shape the dough into 1-inch rounded balls and place 2 inches apart on the prepared baking sheet. Bake for 12-15 minutes, until golden brown.
7. Remove from the oven and cool briefly before transferring the cookies to wire racks. The cookies can be stored in a sealed container for several days.

Hi There, Cookie!

Note: To make gluten-free cookies, use a mixture
such as King Arthur's Measure for Measure or
Cup4Cup from the chefs at The French Laundry.

These are among my most favorite cookies
and my guests loved them, too!

Shirley's Oatmeal Cookies

LYNNETTE SCOFIELD

Makes 3 dozen cookies

Prep Time: 15 minutes ✿ *Baking Time: 12-15 minutes, per baking sheet*

¾ cup soft shortening

1 cup brown sugar

½ cup sugar

1 egg

¼ cup water

1 teaspoon vanilla

1 cup sifted flour

1 teaspoon salt

½ teaspoon baking soda

3 cups dry oats

1 cup chocolate chips, *optional*

¾ cup nuts, *optional*

1 cup dried cranberries, *optional*

1. Preheat oven to 350°. Cover two baking sheets with parchment.
2. Using a stand mixer, place the shortening, sugars, egg, water, and vanilla in its large bowl. Blend together on medium speed.
3. Sift the flour, salt, and baking soda together in a separate bowl. Add to the shortening mixture.
4. Add the oats. Mix on medium speed, scraping the bowl often.
5. If you wish, stir the chocolate chips, nuts, and/or cranberries into the batter.
6. Make 1-inch balls with the dough. Place them on the prepared sheets 2 inches apart.
7. Bake for 12-15 minutes, until the tops are no longer moist and the bottoms are golden brown.

Shirley was my mother and she was a great cook! Not fancy. Just great. I am so happy to have her recipe box, and this recipe was the first one in the Cookie section. It is still a real favorite.

Hi There, Cookie!

Oatmeal Coconut Spice Cookies

YVONNE MARTIN

Makes about 4 dozen cookies

Prep Time: 15 minutes ❧ *Baking Time: 10 minutes, per baking sheet*

1½ cups flour

1½ cups dry quick oats

1 cup sweetened flaked coconut

1 teaspoon baking powder

1 teaspoon baking soda

1½ teaspoons cinnamon

1 teaspoon nutmeg

1 teaspoon ginger

¼ teaspoon dried cloves

1 cup butter-flavored shortening

1 cup sugar

½ cup brown sugar

1 large egg

2 Tablespoons molasses

1 teaspoon vanilla

1. Preheat oven to 325°. Line baking sheets with parchment paper.
2. Combine flour, dry oatmeal, coconut, baking powder, baking soda, and spices (through cloves). Set aside.
3. In a large bowl, cream shortening and the sugars together.
4. Beat in egg, molasses, and vanilla.
5. Add flour mixture and mix together thoroughly.
6. Form dough into 1-inch balls and place on baking sheets 1½ inches apart. (These finished cookies will be about 2½ inches in diameter. For larger cookies, make larger balls and space them further apart on the baking sheets.) Flatten slightly.
7. Bake at 325° for about 10 minutes, or until golden.
8. Remove from the oven and allow to sit on the baking sheets for 10 minutes before transferring to a cooling rack.

Note: In our other recipes, the Broads have always recommended using natural ingredients, such as real butter. But with cookies, the type of fat used affects the texture and shape of the finished product. Cookies made with butter spread thinner and are generally crisper.

We've tried this recipe with both butter and with shortening and prefer the ones made with shortening.

Jeff's Gingersnaps

ELLEN GUTMAN CHENAUX

Makes 20 cookies

Prep Time: 15 minutes ✣ *Chilling Time: 30 minutes*
Baking Time: 10-12 minutes, per baking sheet

12 Tablespoons (1½ sticks)
unsalted butter

¼ cup molasses

1 teaspoon vanilla

2 cups flour

1 cup sugar, plus an extra ½ cup
for coating the cookies, *divided*

2 teaspoons baking soda

2 teaspoons ground ginger

2 teaspoons cinnamon

¼ teaspoon ground nutmeg

¼ teaspoon ground cloves

¼ teaspoon salt

1 egg

1. Melt the butter in a saucepan. Remove from the heat and stir in the molasses and vanilla. Set aside to cool.
2. Sift dry ingredients (from flour through salt) together into a bowl.
3. Stir the egg into the cooled butter mixture.
4. Pour the egg mixture into the dry ingredients. Combine well.
5. Refrigerate for 30 minutes.
6. Preheat the oven to 325°.
7. Pour the remaining ½ cup sugar into a separate bowl. Form the cookie dough into balls about 1 inch in size and roll in the sugar to coat.
8. Place 2 inches apart on the ungreased baking sheet. Bake for 10-12 minutes until the bottoms are starting to brown lightly. You do not want to over-bake them.

Note: These gingersnaps are softer than most traditional ones.

When I was an innkeeper, my first and funniest assistant was Jeff Steinberg. Ironically, when he first arrived, we discovered that we went to the same overnight camp and later to the same college, though years apart. I cherish my many memories of Jeff, including this recipe. And it's a snap!

Hi There, Cookie!

Almond Ginger Cookies

KATHRYN WHITE

Makes 2 dozen large cookies

Prep Time: 15 minutes ❦ *Baking Time: 10 minutes per baking sheet*

2 cups flour

2 teaspoons baking soda

1 teaspoon salt

1 teaspoon cinnamon

1 teaspoon ginger

½ teaspoon allspice

½ teaspoon freshly grated nutmeg

½ teaspoon cloves

¾ cup oil

1 cup sugar

1 large egg

4 Tablespoons molasses

1 teaspoon vanilla

½ cup sliced almonds

1. Preheat the oven to 350°. Line baking sheets with parchment or silicone baking mats.
2. Sift together the flour, baking soda, salt, and spices (through the cloves). Set aside.
3. Using a stand mixer, beat the oil and sugar at medium speed until well blended.
4. Add the egg, molasses, and vanilla and blend.
5. Stir in the dry ingredients and then the almonds until well mixed. The dough will be stiff.
6. Drop the dough by tablespoonfuls onto the baking sheets. Place them 2 inches apart.
7. Bake for 10 minutes.
8. Remove the cookies from the baking sheets and cool.
9. Store in an airtight container with a slice of white bread to preserve the cookies' chewy texture.

These are a favorite to make throughout the fall and holiday season.

Hi There, Cookie!

Pennsylvania Dutch Soft Sugar Cookies

KATHRYN WHITE

Makes 2-3 dozen cookies

Prep Time: 15 minutes ✕ *Baking Time: 8-10 minutes, per baking sheet*

3½ cups flour

2 teaspoons baking powder

1 teaspoon baking soda

1 teaspoon salt

2 cups sugar, plus extra for sprinkling on top of each cookie

16 tablespoons (2 sticks) butter, softened to room temperature

2 large eggs, *divided*

1 Tablespoon vanilla

1 cup buttermilk

1. Preheat the oven to 375°. Line baking sheets with parchment.
2. In a medium-sized bowl, sift together the flour, baking powder, baking soda, and salt. Set aside.
3. In a large bowl, cream together the sugar and butter.
4. Add the eggs one at a time, beating well after each one. Add the vanilla and beat.
5. Stir the flour mixture into the sugar mixture alternating with the buttermilk. Stir until smooth.
6. Drop by tablespoonfuls (or use a small ice cream scoop) 2 inches apart onto the prepared baking sheets. Sprinkle the tops with sugar. Bake for 8-10 minutes, just until the edges are lightly browned.
7. Remove from the baking sheets and cool on a rack. Store in an airtight container with wax paper or parchment separating each layer.

This is a popular cookie in south-central Pennsylvania where I now live. It's very light and cake-like in texture. The story is that the cookie was created by Pennsylvania Dutch folks to use up sour milk, or buttermilk.

Italian Wedding Cookies

LYNNETTE SCOFIELD

Makes about 4 dozen cookies

Prep Time: 45 minutes ❧ *Baking Time: 12-15 minutes, per baking sheet*

3 cups flour

½ teaspoon salt

½ cup sugar

3 teaspoons baking powder

3 Tablespoons butter, melted

3 eggs

½ cup milk

1 teaspoon lemon extract

1 cup confectioners sugar

2 Tablespoons half-and-half

1 teaspoon fresh lemon juice

1. Preheat the oven to 375°. Line a baking sheet with parchment paper.
2. Mix the flour, salt, sugar, and baking powder together well.
3. In a large bowl, cream together the melted butter, eggs, and milk.
4. Stir the dry ingredients into the creamed ones. Stir in the lemon extract, mixing until well blended.
5. When the dough is smooth, make golf-size balls from it. (Flour your hands first as the dough is very sticky.)
6. Place the balls on the baking sheet, 2 inches apart. Bake 12-15 minutes, or until the cookies are firm and turning golden brown around the edges.
7. Cool the cookies before glazing.
8. Combine the confectioners sugar, half-and-half, and lemon juice. Drizzle over the cooled cookies.

If you grew up in central New York in the '50s, you were really familiar with two things: snow and Italian Wedding Cookies. These cookies are still STAPLES at events!

Brown Sugar Drops

LYNNETTE SCOFIELD

Makes 48 cookies

Prep Time: 15 minutes ❧ *Baking Time: 10-15 minutes, per baking sheet*

1 cup firmly packed brown sugar, preferably light brown

20 Tablespoons (2½ sticks) unsalted butter, softened to room temperature

1 teaspoon vanilla

1 egg yolk

2¼ cups flour

1. Preheat oven to 350°.
2. Cover a baking sheet with parchment paper.
3. In large bowl of a stand mixer beat the brown sugar and butter until light and fluffy.
4. Add the vanilla and egg yolk.
5. After blending well, add the flour.
6. Mix until you have a stiff dough.
7. Using two spoons, drop golf-ball-sized balls of dough on the baking sheet, keeping them 1 inch apart.
8. Depending on your oven, bake 10 to 15 minutes, or until the cookies are set. When their bottoms are golden brown, they're done.

That perfect bite when you want "just a little something."

This delicate shortbread-thumbprint cookie
is a big hit year-round. It is one of the most
requested afternoon tea treats at Brampton Inn.

Hi There, Cookie!

Jam Teacakes

DANIELLE HANSCOM THODE

Makes 2 dozen teacakes

Prep Time: 10 minutes ❧ *Baking Time: about 20 minutes, per baking sheet*

16 Tablespoons (2 sticks) unsalted butter, softened to room temperature

½ cup confectioners sugar, sifted, plus more for dusting

1 teaspoon pure vanilla extract

½ teaspoon sea salt

2 cups flour, sifted

½ cup of your favorite preserves, such as orange marmalade, *or* strawberry jam

chopped, toasted nuts, *optional*

1. Preheat the oven to 300°. Line a baking sheet with parchment paper or a silicone liner.
2. Cream the butter with confectioners sugar in the large bowl of a stand mixer.
3. Add the vanilla and salt and mix until well blended.
4. Add the flour and mix just until all of the flour is incorporated. Don't over-mix.
5. Use a 1-inch ice cream scoop to form balls. Place the balls on the baking sheet one inch apart.
6. With your thumb, press down in the center of the ball to form a well. (At this point, the teacakes can be made ahead and frozen for up to 3 months.)
7. Bake for about 20 minutes until golden. (Add approximately 5 minutes when using frozen cookies).
8. Remove from the oven and fill the hot teacakes with a scant teaspoon of the preserves and/or nut topping of your choice. Note: dark jam, such as blueberry, can seep into the baked cookies and stain the edges. They are still delicious but don't look quite as pretty.
9. Carefully move the filled teacakes to a cooling rack.
10. When the teacakes are cool, dust with confectioners sugar.
11. Store in an airtight container for up to 3 days.

Rosemary Lemon Shortbread

DANIELLE HANSCOM THODE

Makes about 48 cookies

Prep Time: 15 minutes 〰 *Chilling Time: 4-8 hours*
Baking Time: 20-25 minutes, per baking sheet

Hi There, Cookie!

2 cups flour

½-¾ teaspoon salt

1 Tablespoon very finely chopped fresh rosemary (do not use dried rosemary)

16 Tablespoons (2 sticks) unsalted butter, softened to room temperature

½ cup confectioners sugar

1½ teaspoons grated lemon zest, from 2 large, well-scrubbed lemons

1. Preheat the oven to 300°. Line baking sheets with parchment paper or silicone mats.
2. Whisk together the flour, salt, and rosemary in a medium-sized bowl. Set aside.
3. Mix together the butter and confectioners sugar in the large bowl of a stand mixer at low speed until smooth and well blended.
4. Add the lemon zest and mix well.
5. Stir in the flour mixture and gently mix until the dough barely holds together.
6. Gather the dough into a ball and transfer to a lightly floured surface. Knead the dough until it just comes together.
7. Divide the dough in half. Form each half into a tight, 8-inch long roll. Refrigerate for 4-8 hours so the dough is thoroughly chilled. (Wrap the dough rolls really well in plastic wrap to freeze them for up to 3 months.)
8. Cut each cold roll into ⅓-inch-thick disks. (The cold dough allows a sharp knife to cut through without crushing the dough and its shape.) Put the disks 1 inch apart on the lined baking sheets.
9. Bake the shortbread in the middle of the oven until barely golden, about 20-25 minutes.
10. Let the cookies cool for 5 minutes. Then move them to a wire rack to cool completely.
11. Shortbread cookies keep in an airtight container at room temperature for up to a week.

These cookies may look unassuming, but they pack a lot of flavor and go well with a glass of iced tea.

Zucchini Cookies

KRISTIE ROSSET

Makes 4 dozen cookies

Prep Time: 45 minutes ❧ *Baking Time: 10 minutes per baking sheet*

3 cups flour

1½ teaspoons baking soda

1 teaspoon baking powder

1½ teaspoons salt

1 Tablespoon cinnamon

1 teaspoon nutmeg

½ teaspoon ground cloves

¾ cup shortening

½ cup sugar

1 cup brown sugar

2 eggs

2 teaspoons vanilla

2 cups peeled and grated zucchini

¾ cup raisins, *or* chopped dates

½ cup chopped pecans, *or* walnuts

2 cups confectioners sugar for the glaze

1. Preheat the oven to 375°. Line a baking sheet with parchment paper.
2. In a medium bowl, whisk the flour, baking soda, baking powder, salt, and spices (through cloves) together. Set aside.
3. Beat the shortening with the sugars until fluffy. Then beat in the eggs and vanilla.
4. Add the dry ingredients alternately with the zucchini three times.
5. Stir in the dates and nuts.
6. Drop by spoonfuls onto the baking sheet, keeping them 2 inches apart.
7. Bake for 10 minutes, or until the edges begin to brown.
8. Remove the cookies from the oven and cool for one minute. Then place the cookies on a wire rack to cool.
9. To make the glaze, whisk the confectioners sugar with small amounts of water until smooth.
10. Drizzle the glaze over the cooled cookies.

What a great way to use zucchini!
These cookies are surprisingly delicious
and a favorite of my daughters.

Foreign Accents

Pear Almond Cake

DANIELLE HANSCOM THODE

Makes 12 servings

Prep Time: 30 minutes ❧ *Baking Time: 45 minutes*

1 cup flour

½ cup almond meal,
or almond flour

2 teaspoons
baking powder

¼ teaspoon fine sea salt

½ teaspoon ground
cardamom

1 teaspoon ground ginger

½ cup brown sugar

1 large egg

6 Tablespoons (¾ stick)
unsalted butter, melted

½ teaspoon
almond extract

4 Tablespoons whole milk

2 ripe Bartlett pears,
peeled, cored, and
each cut into 12 slices

1. Preheat the oven to 350°. Line the bottom of a 9-inch springform pan with parchment paper. Attach the sides of the pan and butter the parchment paper and sides.
2. Sift 1 cup flour, almond meal, baking powder, salt, ½ teaspoon cardamom, and 1 teaspoon ginger together into a large bowl.
3. In a medium bowl, whisk together the brown sugar, egg, 6 Tablespoons melted butter, almond extract, and milk.
4. Pour the egg mixture over the flour mixture and gently mix together with a spatula.
5. Scrape the batter into the prepared springform pan. With a spatula, smooth the top of the batter.
6. Arrange the pear slices in concentric circles over the batter, using all the slices.
7. To make the topping, place 1 cup flour, confectioners sugar, ½ teaspoon cardamom, 1 teaspoon ground ginger, salt, and 8 Tablespoons cold butter into a food processor. Pulse until pea-sized crumbs form.

1 cup flour

½ cup confectioners sugar

½ teaspoon ground cardamom

1 teaspoon ground ginger

¼ teaspoon salt

8 Tablespoons (1 stick) cold unsalted butter, cut in ½-inch-thick pieces

8. Evenly distribute the topping over the pears.
9. Bake for 45 minutes. Check after 35 minutes. If the top is browning too quickly, lower the heat to 325° and cover the cake with a piece of aluminum foil. Insert a toothpick into the center of the cake to see if it might be done. If the pick comes out clean, the cake is finished.
10. Remove from the oven and let cool 10 minutes.
11. Before opening the springform pan, run a thin spatula around the edge to loosen the cake. Remove the rim. Let the cake cool completely on a wire rack.
12. Remove the parchment paper and gently transfer the cake to a plate.

A scrumptious cake.
Perfect with a strong cup of tea!

Arabian Honey Cake

DEBBIE MOSIMANN

Makes 10 servings

Prep Time: 20 minutes ❧ *Baking Time: 27-30 minutes*

The trick is when to put the honey-nut mixture onto the batter. It should happen when the cake is baked enough so that the nuts don't sink to the bottom. But before the cake is baked to the point that the nuts do not adhere and only float on top. You figure this out by trial and error, so don't be discouraged if they sink or float on your first try. The cake is still amazing even if the nuts don't cooperate!

6 Tablespoons
(¾ stick) butter

3 large eggs

⅔ cup sugar

3 Tablespoons
heavy cream

1 teaspoon
vanilla extract

1¼ cups flour

1½ teaspoons
baking powder

7 Tablespoons (nearly
a whole stick) butter

⅓ cup sugar

¼ cup honey

2 Tablespoons
heavy cream

2¼ cups sliced
almonds (6 ounces)

½ teaspoon cinnamon

zest from half an orange

One of my favorite weekday cakes. Full of flavor, easy to put together, and just an all-around winner.

1. Preheat the oven to 375°.
2. Line the bottom of a 10-inch springform pan with parchment. Butter it and the sides of the pan.
3. Melt 6 Tablespoons butter. Set it aside to cool.
4. Whip the eggs and ⅔ cup sugar until light.
5. Stir in the cooled butter, 3 Tablespoons cream, and vanilla.
6. In a separate bowl, add the baking powder to the flour. Distribute and aerate with a wire whisk.
7. Fold the flour mixture into the egg mixture.
8. Pour the batter into the prepared springform. Bake in the middle of the oven for 12-15 minutes or until the top just starts to set.
9. While the batter begins baking, mix 7 Tablespoons butter, ⅓ cup sugar, honey, 2 Tablespoons cream, almonds, cinnamon, and orange zest in a saucepan. Bring to a boil over medium heat.
10. When the cake has partially baked (about 15 minutes), remove the springform pan from the oven and gently distribute the almond mixture over top.
11. Return the cake to the oven. Bake for another 12-15 minutes. Insert a tester into the center of the cake. If it comes out clean, the cake is fully baked.
12. Remove the cake from the oven. Run a knife around the edge to loosen the cake, and then remove the springform pan around it.
13. Place the cake on a cooling rack and finish cooling the cake. Then slide it off the bottom of the pan.

Note: This cake is best served the same day, but it will hold for up to 2 days if put in an airtight container.

Banana Coconut Cake

DEBBIE MOSIMANN

Serves 10-12

Prep Time: 20 minutes ❧ *Baking Time: 40 minutes* ❧ *Cooling Time: 45-60 minutes*

1 banana (a firm one), diced

zest and juice from 1 lemon

16 Tablespoons (2 sticks) butter, softened to room temperature

1½ cups sugar

3 large eggs, *divided*

2 cups flour

2 Tablespoons cornstarch

2 teaspoons baking powder

½ teaspoon baking soda

1 teaspoon salt

¾ cup milk

¾ cup shredded coconut

¼ cup chopped candied ginger

zest from a 2nd lemon

3 Tablespoons fresh juice from the 2nd lemon

1 Tablespoon melted butter

2 cups confectioners sugar

1. Grease and flour an 8-10 cup Bundt pan. Do this well, so that the cake releases easily after baking. Preheat the oven to 350°.
2. In a bowl, combine the diced banana with the zest and juice from one lemon. Set aside.
3. Using a stand mixer, whip the 16 Tablespoons butter and sugar in the large mixing bowl until soft.
4. Add one egg at a time, beating after each addition until batter is light.
5. Measure the flour, cornstarch, baking powder, baking soda, and salt together in a separate bowl. Mix with a whisk to distribute the ingredients evenly.
6. Incorporate the dry ingredients into the egg mixture in two batches, adding alternately with the milk.
7. Fold in the coconut, candied ginger, and the bananas with lemon juice and zest.
8. When everything is well mixed, pour the batter into the prepared pan.
9. Bake for 40 minutes or until a toothpick inserted into the center comes out clean.
10. Remove from the oven and cool for a few minutes.
11. Loosen the cake from the pan with a knife. Then invert onto a cooling rack.

12. Cool completely before glazing.

13. When the cake is nearly cooled, prepare the glaze by mixing together zest and juice from the 2nd lemon, 1 Tablespoon melted butter, and the confectioners sugar. The glaze should be thick but runny. If it is too thick and doesn't drizzle from the spoon, add a few drops of hot water to thin it out. Drizzle over the cooled cake.

The candied ginger in this cake rounds out the flavors.
Bake it a day ahead; it's better the second day.

Nanaimo Bars

KRISTIE ROSSET AND YVONNE MARTIN

Makes 20 servings

Prep Time: 45 minutes ❧ *Chilling Time: 30 minutes*

8 Tablespoons (1 stick) butter, softened to room temperature

¼ cup sugar

1 egg

1 teaspoon vanilla

3 Tablespoons unsweetened cocoa powder

2 cups graham cracker crumbs

1 cup coconut

½ cup finely chopped walnuts or pecans

4 Tablespoons (half a stick) butter, softened to room temperature

3 Tablespoons milk

2 Tablespoons vanilla pudding powder

2 cups confectioners sugar

¾ cup semisweet chocolate chips

1 Tablespoon butter, softened to room temperature

1. Spray a 9 × 9-inch square baking pan with non-stick cooking spray.
2. To make the first layer, mix the 8 Tablespoons softened butter, sugar, egg, vanilla, and cocoa powder in a heat-proof medium bowl. Stir together.
3. In a medium saucepan, bring 2 inches of water to a boil. Set the bowl holding the ingredients in Step 2 over the boiling water, and set the heat to medium. Stir the mixture until slightly thickened, the consistency of pudding. Remove from heat.
4. In a separate bowl stir together the graham cracker crumbs, coconut, and nuts. Add to cocoa mixture and stir well.
5. Pack into the prepared square pan.
6. To make the second layer, mix 4 Tablespoons butter, milk, vanilla pudding powder, and confectioners sugar together well with a stand mixer.
7. Spread over layer one. Refrigerate the filled pan while preparing layer three, allowing the layers to harden a bit.
8. To make the third layer, melt the chocolate in the microwave, stirring every 30 seconds until smooth.

9. Slowly stir in 1 Tablespoon softened butter.
10. Gently spread over layer two.
11. Refrigerate until set. Then cut into 2-inch squares and go crazy!

One of the many benefits I've (Kristie) received from marrying into a Canadian family is this terrific recipe. My mother-in-law prepared this dream of a dessert for every holiday. Whenever we travel to Canada, we find a bakery with Nanaimo Bars. Sinfully good.

And our Canadian Broad, Yvonne, can make them in her sleep!

This bread pudding is much lighter
than more traditional ones.

Foreign Accents

Cherry Bread Pudding (Chriesi Auflauf)

DANIELLE HANSCOM THODE

Makes 12 servings

Prep Time: 25 minutes 🌿 *Baking Time: 60-70 minutes*

1¼ cups whole milk

7 oz. brioche buns (4), *or* muffin bread (crusts removed, and cut into small pieces)

4 large egg yolks (reserve the whites for later)

½ cup + ¾ teaspoon (3 oz.) sugar

1 teaspoon ground cinnamon

1 cup (3½ oz.) finely chopped almonds

2 Tablespoons unbleached flour

1 teaspoon baking powder

4 large egg whites

2 Tablespoons sugar

12-oz. bag of frozen, pitted cherries, *divided*

1. Preheat the oven to 375°. Spray a 10-inch springform pan with non-stick cooking spray.
2. Heat the milk in a large saucepan until it's hot but not boiling.
3. Stir the bread cubes into the milk. Let stand for 15 minutes. The milk should be completely absorbed by the bread.
4. In a large bowl, whisk the egg yolks, sugar, and cinnamon together until very creamy.
5. Stir in the chopped almonds.
6. In a separate bowl, mix the flour and baking powder together. Fold into the egg/almond mixture.
7. Fold in the cooled milk-soaked bread.
8. In a stand mixer beat the egg whites and the 2 Tablespoons of sugar until peaks form. They should be stiff but not dry.
9. Fold ⅓ of the cherries into the bread mixture, followed by ⅓ of the egg whites. Repeat twice.
10. Evenly distribute the mixture in the prepared springform pan. Bake for 60-70 minutes.
11. The bread pudding is done when the top is golden and springy to the touch.
12. Let cool completely before unmolding.

Basler Brunsli

DANIELLE HANSCOM THODE

Makes about 3 dozen cookies
depending on the size of the cookie cutters

Prep Time: 45 minutes ✀ *Chilling Time: overnight, or 8-10 hours*
Baking Time: 10-15 minutes

5 oz. sugar

4 oz. confectioners sugar

9 oz. chopped almonds

3 oz. chopped bittersweet chocolate

1 Tablespoon ground cinnamon

¼ teaspoon salt

¼ teaspoon ground cloves

2 large egg whites

1 teaspoon kirsch, *optional*

sugar for rolling out cookies

1. Cover baking sheets with parchment or silicone mats.
2. Place the sugars, chopped almonds, chopped chocolate, ground cinnamon, salt, and ground cloves into the bowl of a food processor. Grind until very fine.
3. In a small bowl, whisk the egg whites, and kirsch, if you wish. Add to the nut mixture through the feeding tube. Pulse until the dough comes together somewhat. (It is a wet dough.)
4. Put a large piece of parchment paper on the work surface and sprinkle with a small amount of sugar.
5. Remove the dough from the food processor and divide it in two. Pat the first dough into a ball, sprinkle with a bit more sugar, and roll it out to ¼" thickness.
6. Repeat with the second half.
7. To cut out the cookies, use simple 2-inch cookie cutter shapes, such as a circle, square, half-moon, etc.
8. The dough is delicate. Place the cookies carefully on the covered baking sheets, 2 inches apart.
9. Refrigerate uncovered overnight. This is very important!

10. In the morning, preheat the oven to 300°. Bake the cold cookies for 10-15 minutes.
11. Remove the cookies from the oven when they're dry but still soft. Then carefully move the warm cookies to a wire rack. Let them cool completely before serving or storing.
12. These fragrant cookies can be stored in a cookie tin for up to a week.

A Swiss chocolate–almond–spice cookie for the holiday season. And, yes, you'll need a cooking scale for this recipe.

Linzer Torte

DEBBIE MOSIMANN

Makes 8-10 servings

Prep Time: 75 minutes ✥ *Baking Time: 40-50 minutes*

The Linzer torte's origins are from a small city that lies along the beautiful Danube River in Austria. Having spent a summer on the outskirts of this beautiful city, I can tell you the bakeries are downright amazing, and everyone has a slightly different variation of their namesake torte. The chocolate in this one rounds out the flavors.

16 Tablespoons butter
(2 sticks), softened to
room temperature

1 cup sugar

2 large eggs, beaten
(save about 1 Tablespoon
to brush on the top)

8 oz. almond flour

¼ cup grated dark chocolate

1 Tablespoon lemon zest

1 Tablespoon fresh
lemon juice

¼ teaspoon baking powder

¼ teaspoon baking soda

½ teaspoon cinnamon

pinch of cloves

pinch of ginger

pinch of salt

1⅓ cups flour

⅔ cup red raspberry
jam, *or* red currant jam

3 Tablespoons flour,
reserved to mix into
the last ¼ of dough

1. In a mixing bowl, cream the butter with the sugar. Add the beaten eggs a bit at a time, mixing until fluffy. Reserve 1 tablespoon of the egg to brush on the top at the end.
2. Add the almond flour, grated chocolate, lemon zest and juice, baking powder, baking soda, cinnamon, cloves, ginger, salt, and flour. Mix until well combined.
3. Cover the bottom of a 9-inch springform pan with parchment. Butter it and the sides of the pan. Spread ¾ of the batter into the pan.
4. Stir the jam to loosen it up. Drop it in small dollops over the batter, and then spread it gently to within ½ inch of the edge.
5. Preheat the oven to 375°.
6. Add the 2 reserved tablespoons of flour to the remaining ¼ batter. You need to make a soft dough that you can roll. Roll to ½-inch thick.
7. Using a knife, gently cut strips of dough about 1 inch wide and 9¼ inches long. I use a ruler to help as a guide.
8. Weave a basket weave pattern over the dough, crisscrossing the jam. Don't worry if it's not perfect. It will bake together and look just fine!
9. Brush the top with the remaining whisked egg.
10. Bake 40-50 minutes, but begin checking at 35 minutes. The cake will be done when a toothpick inserted into the center comes out clean and the cake pulls away from the sides of the pan.
11. Remove the cake from the oven. Run a knife around the edge of the pan and pull off the rim of the springform. Cool on a rack.
12. When completely cool, use a cake spatula to remove the bottom plate.

Sticky Toffee Pudding

KATHRYN WHITE

Makes 12 servings

Prep Time: 30 minutes ✂ *Baking Time: 40-45 minutes* ✂ *Cooling Time: 2 hours*

2 cups pitted and chopped dates (about 12 ounces)

2¼ cups water

2 teaspoons baking soda

3¼ cups flour (I use King Arthur Gluten Free Measure for Measure)

1 Tablespoon baking powder

½ teaspoon cinnamon

½ teaspoon salt

8 Tablespoons (1 stick) butter, softened to room temperature

2 cups sugar

4 large eggs, *divided*

1 teaspoon vanilla

1 cup brown sugar

8 Tablespoons (1 stick) butter

1 cup heavy cream

1 teaspoon vanilla

whipped cream, *optional*

1. Preheat the oven to 350°. Butter a 9 × 13-inch baking pan.
2. Place the dates and water in a small saucepan and bring to a boil over high heat. Continue simmering for 5 minutes. Remove the pan from the heat and stir in the baking soda (it will foam). Set aside.
3. In a medium bowl combine the flour, baking powder, cinnamon, and salt. Whisk to blend the ingredients. Set aside.
4. Using a hand mixer, cream the softened 8 Tablespoons butter before adding the sugar; then cream both until fluffy.
5. Add the eggs one at a time. Add 1 teaspoon vanilla and blend. Be sure to scrape the bowl as needed.
6. Add about ⅓ of the flour mixture and ⅓ of the dates to the creamed mixture. Blend on low. Continue adding the flour and the dates alternately, until everything is incorporated into the batter.
7. Pour the batter into the baking pan. Bake 40-45 minutes (gluten-free flour generally takes about 5 minutes longer to bake than regular all-purpose flour). The cake should be firm and set in the center.

8. Let the cake cool in the pan on a wire rack.
9. Meanwhile, combine the brown sugar, 8 Tablespoons butter, and heavy cream in a saucepan. Bring to a boil while stirring. Simmer for an additional minute or two until the sauce is blended and smooth. Remove from the heat and stir in 1 teaspoon vanilla.
10. Serve by spooning the sauce onto individual dessert plates and placing a slice of cake on top of each one. You can spoon additional sauce over the cake. Top with whipped cream if desired.

I first got hooked on this sweet treat at The Schlafly Tap Room in St. Louis. Considered a traditional English dessert, it is a dense, moist cake that sits in a pool of warm, caramel toffee sauce.

Chocolate and poached pears are
a match made in heaven!

Poire Hélène

DANIELLE HANSCOM THODE

Makes 4 servings

Prep Time: 40 minutes ❧ *Cooking Time: 25-30 minutes* ❧ *Cooling Time: 1-2 hours*

4 small Bartlett pears, ripe but not mushy (or they won't hold their shape), with stems on

3 cups water

2 cups sugar

peel and juice from 3 oranges

¼ cup Grand Marnier

6 oz. bittersweet chocolate

4 oz. heavy cream

1 Tablespoon Grand Marnier

1. Peel the pears, being careful not to cut the stem.
2. With an apple corer, remove the core of the pears from the bottom, leaving the pear and stem intact.
3. In a tall saucepan, bring the water, sugar, orange peel, orange juice, and ¼ cup Grand Marnier to a low simmer. Let simmer 5 minutes.
4. Add the pears, making sure the pears can stand upright and are covered with the poaching liquid. Add more water if necessary.
5. Cover and simmer on low 15 to 20 minutes. Check the pears with a sharp knife regularly. When finished cooking, they should still be slightly firm.
6. Remove the orange peel. Let the pears cool completely in the poaching syrup.
7. The pears can be poached up to 2 days ahead and kept in the poaching syrup in the refrigerator.
8. When ready to serve, remove the pears from the poaching syrup. Let drip on a wire rack.
9. Heat the chocolate, heavy cream, and 1 Tablespoon Grand Marnier in a medium saucepan. Whisk until the chocolate is melted.
10. Dip each pear at an angle into the chocolate sauce. Do not immerse completely. Set neatly on a dessert plate and serve.

Scottish Shortbread

YVONNE MARTIN

Makes about 40 pieces

Prep Time: 15 minutes ❧ *Chilling Time: 15 minutes* ❧ *Baking Time: 45 minutes*

1 pound butter (4 sticks),
softened to room temperature

1 cup sugar

3½ cups flour

½ cup rice flour

2 Tablespoons sanding, *or*
regular, sugar, *optional*

Everyone thinks their grandma has the best shortbread recipe ever. The final result of this very traditional version is similar to the Scottish shortbread sold in tins at Christmas-time. The rice flour gives a crisp-tender mouth feel. For an interesting variation, you can mix ¼ cup chopped crystallized ginger with the flour.

1. Preheat the oven to 275°.
2. Use a small baking sheet (11 × 15-inch), or two 9 × 9-inch square baking pans. Do not grease.
3. Cream the butter and sugar together in a large bowl.
4. Mix in the flours until barely combined.
5. Place the dough directly onto the cookie sheet and knead lightly.
6. Press the dough with your fingers to evenly cover the cookie sheet. Prick with a fork at 2-inch intervals. Refrigerate for 15 minutes.
7. Bake the shortbread until golden brown, about 45 minutes.
8. As soon as the shortbread comes out of the oven, dust it with sanding sugar or regular sugar. Shake the pan to spread the sugar evenly over the top.
9. Using a sharp knife, cut the shortbread into 2-inch squares while it is still warm.
10. Let the shortbread cool on the baking sheet.
11. Store in an airtight container.

Note: Don't skip the refrigerated rest time—it makes the shortbread crisp and tender.

Tutti Fruitti

Caramel Apple Walnut Squares

YVONNE MARTIN

Makes 12 servings

Prep Time: 15 minutes *Baking Time: 30-35 minutes*

about 20 soft caramels

1¾ cups flour

1 cup dry quick oats

½ cup brown sugar

½ teaspoon baking soda

½ teaspoon salt

16 Tablespoons (2 sticks) butter, chilled

14-oz. can sweetened condensed milk

20-oz. can apple pie filling

1 cup chopped walnuts

ice cream, *or* whipped cream

1. Preheat oven to 375°. Lightly spray a 9 × 13-inch baking pan. Unwrap the caramels. Try not to eat too many.
2. In a large mixing bowl, combine the flour, oats, brown sugar, baking soda, and salt.
3. Cut the butter into ½-inch cubes. Using a pastry cutter or 2 sharp knives, cut the butter into the flour mixture until crumbs form and no butter chunks remain. (You can also do this in a food processor, cutting the butter into the dry ingredients.)
4. Set aside 1½ cups of the crumb mixture. Press the remaining crumbs into the bottom of the prepared pan.
5. Bake at 375° for 15 minutes.
6. While the crust is baking, pour the condensed milk into a medium saucepan. Add the caramels. Cook over low heat, stirring constantly until the caramels are melted. Watch carefully. This mixture burns very easily.
7. Spoon the apple pie filling evenly over the baked crust. Spread the caramel mixture over the apples.

Tutti Fruitti

8. Mix the walnuts with the reserved crumb mixture. Sprinkle this over the caramel mixture. Return to the oven and bake for 15 to 20 minutes until the top is golden and firm.

9. Allow to cool for about 15 minutes before serving. Cut into 12 squares and serve with ice cream or whipped cream.

An inn guest shared this recipe with me many years ago. Since then we've served it at the inn for dessert dozens of times, always to rave reviews.

Roasted Pears with Outrageous Crumble

ELLEN GUTMAN CHENAUX

Makes 4 servings

Prep Time: 10 minutes

*Roasting Time: 30-42 minutes (10-12 minutes for the crumble;
20-30 minutes for the pears, and during half that time
you can roast the nuts and seeds with the pears)*

There are an infinite number of incredible
crumble toppings, but this topping,
paired with pears (not peared with pairs!)
is the queen of crumble! It brings pears
to new heights, and if you are feeling
decadent, try it on ice cream. When I was
an innkeeper, this was our most-requested
recipe. Try it and you'll know why!

2 ripe but still quite firm pears (I recommend Bartlett *or* Anjou)

2 teaspoons, plus 2 Tablespoons, olive oil, *divided*

¼ cup almonds, *or* pecans, chopped

¼ cup shelled pumpkin seeds

2 Tablespoons brown sugar

2 Tablespoons dry old-fashioned oats

pinch of kosher salt

1 Tablespoon black sesame seeds

½ cup mascarpone

2 teaspoons sugar

1. Preheat the oven to 375°.
2. Cut the pears in half lengthwise and core them.
3. Place the pears cut side up on a baking sheet.
4. Drizzle the pears with 2 teaspoons of olive oil.
5. Bake on the upper rack of the oven until the pears are softened but not mushy, about 20-30 minutes. They're done if they're slightly tender when poked with a fork or sharp knife. Do not overbake.
6. When the pears begin roasting, you can toss the nuts, pumpkin seeds, brown sugar, dry oats, salt, and 2 Tablespoons oil together.
7. Spoon onto a baking sheet. Place in the oven with the pears, putting the crumble mixture on the lower rack and stirring occasionally. Bake until golden brown, about 10-12 minutes.
8. Remove the baking sheet with the seasoned nuts and pumpkin seeds from the oven. Stir in the sesame seeds.
9. Set aside to cool.
10. Meanwhile, mix the mascarpone and sugar together in a small bowl.
11. To serve, spoon a quarter of the mascarpone-sugar mixture onto each plate. Place a pear half on top of the mascarpone. Top with the crumble. Serve and you'll soon hear the angels sing!

A clafouti is a traditional French dessert often made with black cherries. It is typically served warm with a dusting of confectioners sugar, or with cream, and can be made with blueberries, apples, pears, plums, or peaches.

Tutti Fruitti

Peach Clafouti

KATHRYN WHITE

Makes 8 servings

Prep Time: 20 minutes ❧ *Baking Time: 30–40 minutes* ❧ *Cooling Time: 15-20 minutes*

2 large peaches,
peeled and sliced

½ teaspoon
ground ginger

½ teaspoon cinnamon

¾ cup heavy cream

¾ cup half-and-half

1 teaspoon
vanilla extract

4 large eggs

½ cup sugar

½ cup flour, sifted

1. Preheat oven to 375°. Butter or spray a tart pan or 10-inch pie plate with non-stick cooking spray.
2. Place the peaches on the bottom of the baking dish. Blueberries, apples, and cherries (without pits) are also a tasty option.
3. Sprinkle ginger and cinnamon over the peaches. Adjust your choice of seasonings if you use fruit other than peaches (nutmeg and cinnamon go well with apples, for example).
4. Combine the heavy cream and half-and-half in a saucepan. Heat over medium setting until the mixture almost boils. Remove from the heat. Stir in the vanilla. Let the cream mixture cool.
5. While the cream mixture cools, lightly beat the eggs in a medium-sized bowl. Gradually add the sugar, whisking until blended.
6. Add the flour to the egg mixture, a little at a time, until thoroughly incorporated.
7. Add the cream mixture to the eggs and sugar. Whisk constantly as you slowly add the cream mixture, to create a custard.
8. Pour the custard over the peaches and place the dish in the oven. Bake 30–40 minutes (the time will vary depending upon how shallow the baking dish is), or until the custard is set. The custard will puff up and then settle, which is normal.
9. Let it cool 15–20 minutes and then serve.

Baked Pears with Vanilla Cream Cheese Sauce

JOYCE SCHULTE

Makes 6 – 8 servings

Prep Time: 30 minutes (Sauce: 15 minutes; Pears and nuts: 15 minutes)

Bake Time: 25 minutes for ripe pears; 40 minutes for firm or under-ripe pears

½ cup soft cream cheese spread (in a tub; not whipped; not a block)

2 Tablespoons honey

1 teaspoon vanilla extract

¼ teaspoon nutmeg

3-4 pears (preferably Anjou *or* Bartlett)

4 Tablespoons brown sugar

½ cup orange juice

¼ teaspoon ground cloves (use ⅛ teaspoon if you do not like a strong clove taste)

½ teaspoon vanilla

½ teaspoon cinnamon

chopped pecans, *optional*

1. Prepare the sauce in a small bowl by combining cream cheese, honey, vanilla extract, and nutmeg until well blended. Set aside.
2. Preheat the oven to 350°. Grease a 9-inch pie plate or glass baking dish.
3. Peel, core, and cut pears in half lengthwise. Arrange in the pie plate or baking dish, cut side down.
4. Combine the brown sugar, orange juice, cloves, vanilla, and cinnamon. Pour over the pears.
5. Bake, uncovered, 25-40 minutes. Baste the pears with the liquid once or twice while they bake. Their length of baking time depends on how ripe they are. They're finished when they're slightly tender when poked with a fork or sharp knife. Do not overbake them.

Tutti Fruitti

6. Place pears on a serving dish, cut side up. Spoon the cream cheese sauce into each pear half. Drizzle with any remaining liquid and top with chopped pecans if you wish.

Cooked pears are just so incredibly good! Add the cream cheese sauce and you have a great dessert.

Raspberry Kiwi Trifle

DANIELLE HANSCOM THODE

Makes 12 servings

Prep Time: 25 minutes

1 pound cake
(see recipe on page 48)

¼ cup simple syrup
(heat ¼ cup water and
¼ cup sugar, stirring
continuously until
sugar is completely
dissolved)

¼ cup Grand Marnier

1 recipe vanilla custard
(see recipe on page 214)

3 half-pints fresh
raspberries, *divided* *

3 large, ripe but
still firm, kiwis

1 cup cold heavy cream

½ Tablespoon sugar

** Reserve a half-pint
of the best-looking
raspberries to
decorate the top.*

1. Cut pound cake into nine ½"-thick slices. Remove crust. Set slices aside.
2. In a 1-cup measuring cup blend the simple syrup and Grand Marnier. Set aside.
3. Peel and slice the kiwis into ¼-inch-thick slices. Set aside.
4. Place a layer of cake in the bottom of a 2½- to 3-quart glass (preferably footed) trifle dish. Cut into pieces to fit.
5. Sprinkle with ⅓ of simple syrup mixture. Then spoon ¾ cup of the vanilla custard over the cake. Try not to spoon the custard too close to the edge of the bowl so everyone can see into the sides of the trifle.
6. Arrange 1 half-pint of raspberries over top.
7. Repeat the 3 layers: cake, simple syrup mixture, and custard.
8. Top with kiwi slices, arranged overlapping in concentric circles.
9. Add the third layer of cake, simple syrup mixture, custard, and another half-pint of raspberries.
10. Whip the heavy cream in the bowl of a stand mixer fitted with a whisk attachment. When it starts to thicken, add ½ Tablespoon of sugar. Continue to whip until stiff peaks form. (Don't overdo it or you'll have butter.)
11. Decorate the trifle with the whipped cream. Top with the reserved raspberries.
12. Refrigerate until ready to serve.

Strawberry Shortcake

KATHRYN WHITE

Makes 6 to 8 shortcakes

Prep Time: 10 minutes ✣ Baking Time: 12 minutes

2 cups flour

3 teaspoons baking powder

¼ teaspoon salt

¼ cup sugar

6 Tablespoons (¾ stick) butter, cold, and cut into small pieces

1 large egg

⅓ cup half-and-half

1 quart strawberries, rinsed, hulled, and sliced

sugar for sprinkling on shortcakes, plus ¼ cup sugar for strawberries

1 cup heavy cream

¼ teaspoon vanilla

1. Preheat oven to 425°. Place a silicone baking mat on a baking sheet and set aside. Chill a small bowl and beaters in the freezer for making the whipped cream topping.
2. In a medium bowl, combine the flour, baking powder, salt, and ¼ cup sugar.
3. Add the butter to the bowl. Cut it into the flour with a pastry cutter until the mixture forms crumbs.
4. In a small bowl whisk together the egg and half-and-half. Add to the flour mixture. Stir until just blended and the flour is moistened.
5. Transfer dough to a lightly floured surface and knead 2 to 3 times. Pat the dough to a ½-inch thickness. Cut out rounds with a 2½-inch biscuit cutter. Collect the scraps of dough and pat together. Cut more rounds until the dough is completely used and you have 6 to 8 rounds.
6. Place the rounds on the baking sheet. Sprinkle a little sugar on top if each one.
7. Bake 12 minutes or until golden brown.
8. While the shortcakes are baking, toss the strawberries together with ¼ cup sugar in a medium bowl.
9. Remove the small bowl and beaters from the freezer. Place the heavy cream and vanilla in the bowl and beat on high with a stand mixer. Refrigerate until ready to use.
10. Split hot biscuits in half, spoon strawberries over the bottom half, top with whipped cream, and cover with the second half-biscuit. Serve immediately.

When strawberries are in season, what could be better?
Try the recipe below and you will never settle for buying the
overly sweet concoctions found in the grocery store.

Tutti Fruitti

Heavenly Bananas

JOYCE SCHULTE

Makes 4 servings

Prep Time: 10 minutes ❧ Resting Time for sauce: 8-10 hours

½ cup sour cream (regular, not "lite")

2 Tablespoons sugar

1 Tablespoon orange juice

½ teaspoon grated orange peel

4 bananas

suggested toppings: dried cranberries, fresh raspberries, chopped strawberries, and/ or shaved chocolate

1. About 8-10 hours before serving, mix the sour cream, sugar, orange juice, and orange peel together.
2. Cover tightly and refrigerate. (Note, the sauce will keep just fine in the refrigerator for a full 24 hours.)
3. When you're ready to serve, slice bananas and place in serving bowls.
4. Stir the sour cream mixture. Top each dish of bananas with 1-2 Tablespoons of the sauce.
5. Sprinkle with the topping(s) of your choice. Shaved chocolate and raspberries make this a great dessert.

This was a great favorite at our bed and breakfast. For breakfast we topped it with dried cranberries in winter, or with fresh raspberries in summer. Both go well with the orange flavor. A guest gave me the idea to think of it as dessert after she told me she served it at a dinner party, topped with shaved chocolate. It's a delicious, light, sweet way to end a meal.

Strawberry Rhubarb Compote

JOYCE SCHULTE

Makes 6 servings

Prep Time: 10 minutes ✻ *Cooking Time: 30-40 minutes*

fresh, *or* frozen, rhubarb
cut into chunks

3 cups frozen
strawberries

½ cup sugar

1 Tablespoon water

whipped cream
for garnish

1. Put the rhubarb, strawberries, sugar, and water in a large heavy cooking pot.
2. Cook 30-40 minutes over medium heat, stirring frequently. The fruit should be fairly well broken down and soft. Consistency should be similar to applesauce but not soupy. A few small chunks of fruit are fine.
3. If the mixture is too thin, add some cornstarch to thicken. Taste, and add more sugar if it is too tart.
4. Allow to cool.
5. Serve in small dishes (6-ounce ramekins work well) with whipped cream on top. Or use the compote to fill crepes, or to top pancakes, waffles, or vanilla ice cream.

This is a great flavor combination, with the sweetness of the strawberries and the tartness of the rhubarb. It just feels like summer. Make a batch, eat some of it now, and freeze the rest to have on hand for a quick topping any time of the year. This recipe doubles easily and freezes well.

Fruit Pizza

KRISTIE ROSSET

Makes 12-16 servings

Prep Time: 30-45 minutes ❧ *Chilling Time: 60 minutes for dough*
Baking Time: 20 minutes

Stunning presentation, and delicious, too.

1 teaspoon
baking soda

½ teaspoon salt

1 cup sour cream

16 Tablespoons
(2 sticks) butter,
melted

2 cups sugar

2 eggs

1 teaspoon vanilla

5 cups flour

8-oz. package cream
cheese, softened

⅓ cup sugar

peaches, peeled
and sliced

kiwi, peeled
and sliced

fresh strawberries,
washed, dried,
and halved

fresh blueberries,
raspberries,
blackberries—
your choice

4 Tablespoons
(¼ cup) apple jelly

1. Preheat oven to 350°.
2. To make the sugar cookie base, stir the baking soda and salt into the sour cream. Set aside.
3. Cream the butter and 2 cups sugar in the bowl of a stand mixer until thoroughly incorporated.
4. Add the eggs and vanilla to the mixer bowl and mix well.
5. Add the sour cream mixture to the bowl and beat on low until smooth.
6. Gradually add the flour, beating on low speed, until fully incorporated.
7. Form the dough into two balls, wrap in wax paper, and chill for one hour or more before handling.
8. Using the palm of your hand, press one chilled dough ball onto a 15-inch round baking stone or pizza pan, leaving a one-inch space around the edge of the pan. (Freeze the extra dough ball for later use, including making cookies.) The dough should be about ¼ inch thick. (If it's too thick, it will spill over the pan while baking).
9. If you choose to simplify* and use refrigerated dough, press it onto the pizza pan, following the directions above.
10. Bake the crust for approximately 20 minutes, or until it is a light golden brown. Allow to cool completely.
11. For the "sauce," combine the cream cheese and ⅓ cup sugar in a small bowl using a hand mixer. Spread the mixture evenly over the cooled pizza crust.
12. Prepare the fruit and arrange in any lovely fashion you want over the cream cheese.
13. In a microwave, melt the apple jelly until liquid. Using a pastry brush, gently brush a thin layer of the apple jelly over the fruit to provide a glaze and keep the fruit from turning brown.
14. Refrigerate until ready to serve.

Note: To simplify, you can use a 16-oz. package refrigerated sugar cookie dough, and skip Steps 2-7 above.

Pineapple, Mangoes, and Thyme

JOYCE SCHULTE

Makes 10 1-cup servings

Prep Time: 20 minutes ✻ *Chilling Time: 1 hour or more*

1 large fresh pineapple, cut into 1-inch cubes

2 large ripe mangoes, cut into bite-sized pieces

2 Tablespoons fresh lime juice (add more to taste if you wish)

1 Tablespoon fresh thyme leaves*

* Or more if you really like thyme. Leaves only, no stems.

1. Mix pineapple chunks and mango pieces in a large bowl.
2. Add lime juice and fresh thyme and mix well.
3. Taste and add more thyme or lime juice to suit your taste.
4. Refrigerate for at least an hour before serving.

I first enjoyed this at a friend's home. I'm not really fond of mangoes, but she said, "Just wait. Paired with the thyme, even you will like this." She was right. It is delicious and makes a great light summer dessert.

Cool It

Fudge Sundae Frozen Goodness

KRISTIE ROSSET

Makes 20 servings

Prep Time: 60 minutes ✸ *Baking Time: 20 minutes* ✸ *Freezing Time: at least 4 hours*

3 egg whites

1 cup sugar

1 teaspoon baking powder

1 teaspoon white vinegar

½ cup chopped pecans

crumbs from 16 saltine crackers*

1 cup evaporated milk

1 cup miniature marshmallows

1 cup semisweet chocolate chips

1 teaspoon salt

½ gallon vanilla ice cream, *divided* (some will be left over)

½ cup coarsely chopped pecans

* Put the crackers in a large Ziploc baggie; use a rolling pin or wine bottle to crush them. Or crush them in your food processor.

1. Preheat the oven to 325°. Grease a 9 x 13-inch baking pan with non-stick cooking spray.
2. Prepare the soda cracker crust by beating the egg whites until stiff peaks form. Beat the sugar into the egg whites.
3. Add the baking powder and vinegar and beat to incorporate. Stir in the pecans. Add the cracker crumbs and mix all together.
4. Pour the crust batter into the prepared baking dish. Smooth the batter.
5. Bake until slightly golden, about 20 minutes. Then cool completely.
6. To make the sundae, place the evaporated milk, marshmallows, chocolate chips, and salt in a medium saucepan.
7. Stir over medium heat until the ingredients are melted and smooth. Continue to stir, cooking until thickened to the consistency of soft pudding.

8. Remove from the heat and cool to room temperature.
9. Soften the ice cream until it's easily spoonable and spreadable. Spoon up to half the ice cream over the cooled soda cracker crust, creating a layer about ½-1 inch thick.
10. Next, layer half the chocolate mixture over the ice cream.
11. Repeat with another layer of ice cream, and then a layer of the remaining chocolate mixture.
12. Sprinkle with pecans and freeze until firm, at least 4 hours.
13. Cut into 20 squares and serve.

Frozen comfort food. I promise. Try varying
the type of ice cream to suit your
taste or the season, such as peppermint
ice cream for the holidays.

San Francisco Mud Pie,
Inspired by MacArthur Park Restaurant

ELLEN GUTMAN CHENAUX

Makes 8-10 servings

Prep time: 30 minutes (crust, 5 minutes; filling, 10 minutes; sauce, 15 minutes)

Freezing time: 3-8 hours, or overnight, the longer the better

I first saw this recipe in The Toronto Star in 1976 and have served it to friends and family for years. In the mid-2000s, when I was publishing my inn's cookbook, I called the MacArthur Park Restaurant (yes, it's THAT MacArthur Park!) and asked for permission to reprint the recipe. Their response? "Lady, if you've had this recipe for 30 years, it's all yours."

2½ cups rich chocolate
ice cream

2½ cups coffee ice cream

8-10 chocolate
chip cookies*

5 Tablespoons butter

2 Tablespoons
boiling water

1 Tablespoon instant
espresso powder

¼ cup Kahlua, *or* any
coffee *or* chocolate liqueur

4 oz. bittersweet
baking chocolate
(good quality, such as
Callebaut), chopped

4 Tablespoons
(half a stick) unsalted
butter, cut in chunks

1½ cups sugar

½ cup heavy cream

⅛ cup light corn syrup

1 teaspoon vanilla extract

chocolate curls, *optional*

** homemade, Chips Ahoy,
or another brand of
packaged chocolate
chip cookies*

1. Set out the ice creams so they begin to soften.
2. Chill a 10-inch pie plate in the freezer while you make the crust.
3. In a food processor, pulse the cookies until coarsely chopped. Add the butter. Pulse in one-second bursts until the cookies and butter form a crumbly paste (5-8 seconds). The paste should be coarse, not smooth.
4. Firmly pat the cookie-butter paste into the chilled pie plate to form a crust over the bottom and up the sides.
5. Return the pie plate to the freezer.
6. When the ice creams are soft enough to beat, spoon them into the bowl of a stand mixer.
7. Start the mixer on slow, slowly increasing to medium speed until the ice creams are well blended.
8. Blend the espresso powder into the boiling water until dissolved. Then add it and the liqueur to the mixer bowl. Run the mixer just long enough to incorporate these ingredients.
9. Spoon the mixture into the frozen pie shell. Cover the pie loosely with plastic wrap. Freeze for 3-8 hours (preferably overnight) until the pie filling is fairly solid.
10. In the top of a double boiler, over simmering (not boiling) water, combine the chopped baking chocolate, butter, sugar, cream, and corn syrup. Stir continuously until the mixture is completely melted and smooth.
11. Increase the heat to medium and bring the mixture just to a boil. Simmer for 10 minutes.
12. Remove the chocolate mixture from the stove. Stir in the vanilla.
13. Pour the sauce into a microwave-safe bowl, cover, and store in the refrigerator.
14. Just before serving the pie, reheat the sauce in the microwave for 3-4 minutes, stirring halfway through, until the sauce is just-hot.
15. Pour over the mud pie, or over each slice as you serve. Add chocolate curls to the top if you wish.

Strawberry Ice Cream Roll

DEBBIE MOSIMANN

Makes 12 slices

Prep Time: 30 minutes ❧ *Baking Time: 12-15 minutes* ❧ *Freezing Time: several hours*

3 eggs

¾ cup sugar

zest from half an orange
(reserve the orange for its juice)

¾ cup flour

¾ teaspoon baking powder

¼ teaspoon baking soda

¼ teaspoon salt

¼ cup orange juice

1 teaspoon vanilla

confectioners sugar

½ gallon good quality
strawberry ice cream

½ cup fresh strawberry jam

1 Tablespoon water,
or orange liqueur

whipped cream

fresh, *or* macerated,
strawberries and fresh
mint leaves to garnish

1. Preheat the oven to 375°. Line a 15 × 10-inch jelly roll pan with parchment paper. Spray with a non-stick spray or grease and flour the paper.
2. In a mixing bowl beat the eggs until they are lemon yellow. Gradually add the sugar and then the orange zest.
3. In a separate bowl mix the flour, baking powder, baking soda, and salt. Whisk to combine.
4. Add the flour mixture gradually to the eggs and sugar using a stand mixer.
5. When well mixed, blend in the orange juice and vanilla.
6. Scrape the bowl well and then pour the batter onto the prepared jelly roll pan.
7. Bake for 12-15 minutes, or until the cake springs back to a gentle touch.
8. While the cake is baking, place a linen (not microfiber or terry) tea towel on the counter. Sprinkle it well with confectioners sugar (you may wish to use a sieve to do this).
9. When the cake comes out of the oven, let it cool slightly. Then loosen the sides and turn it upside down on the towel.
10. Remove the parchment paper gently.
11. From the long side, roll the cake (along with the tea towel) into a log. Set aside to cool.

This dessert is so much easier than it sounds and always makes a statement. Use the best strawberry ice cream that you can find and make sure it is soft enough to spread evenly. The Roll can be frozen for weeks.

12. Place the ice cream in the refrigerator so it can temper and be soft enough to spread without melting.
13. When the cake is cool, gently unroll it, removing the towel.
14. Whisk the strawberry preserves with a tablespoon of water or orange liquor. Spread onto the cake in a very thin layer.
15. Take the ice cream from the refrigerator. Taking thin slabs from the side of the container with a spatula, spread the ice cream in a layer about an inch or more thick across the strawberry preserves.

16. When finished, reroll the filled cake into a large log again. Place on a baking sheet, cover with plastic wrap, and freeze for several hours until you are ready to serve.
17. About 30 minutes before you're ready to serve the roll, remove it from the freezer. Place in the refrigerator to temper for half an hour or less.
18. Slice into 1½-inch-thick slices.
19. Garnish with whipped cream, strawberries, and mint leaves. Serve immediately.

Cool It

Strawberry Popsicles

DEBBIE MOSIMANN AND KRISTIE ROSSET

Serves: 24 or more, depending upon the size of the molds

Prep Time: 15 minutes   Freezing Time: 4 hours, or overnight

1½ quarts hulled and halved strawberries

4 cups low-fat buttermilk, *divided*

¼ cup sugar

⅔ cup sour cream

3 Tablespoons apple juice

1. In the large bowl of a food processor (or do two processes in a smaller bowl), blend the strawberries, 1 cup buttermilk, and sugar. Leaving some strawberries in small chunks creates a prettier popsicle, but it's fine to pulverize them all. Set the mixture aside.
2. Combine the remaining 3 cups buttermilk, sour cream, and apple juice in a large bowl.
3. Pour the strawberry mixture into the sour cream mixture. Whisk to combine thoroughly.
4. Pour into popsicle molds so they're about ⅔ full. Put the popsicle sticks in place.
5. Freeze for several hours or overnight.

Or just pour our famous strawberry soup into popsicle molds and freeze. Voila! A refreshing and healthy treat, chock full of strawberries.

Gin & Tonic Popsicles

ELLEN GUTMAN CHENAUX

Makes 6-8 servings

Prep Time: 15 minutes ❧ *Freezing Time: 12-24 hours*

3 cups tonic water

1½ oz. gin (If you don't like gin, try vodka.)

juice from half a lime

⅓ cup sugar

¼ cup lime zest

½ cup lime slices

1. Mix all of the ingredients together except the lime slices.
2. Place the lime slices into popsicle molds and pour the other ingredients into the molds.
3. Freeze the popsicles for 12-24 hours. Serve and enjoy!

Note: You will need popsicle molds.

These are so cool! Popsicles for adults!
A great way to enjoy summer!

Key Lime Pie

ELLEN GUTMAN CHENAUX

Makes 8 servings

Prep Time: 15 minutes

Baking Time: 25-27 minutes (10-12 minutes for the crust; 15 minutes for the pie)

Cooling time: 45-50 minutes (15 minutes for the crust; 30-40 minutes for the pie)

Chilling Time: 3 hours or more

5⅓ Tablespoons unsalted butter

1¼ cups graham cracker crumbs

3 Tablespoons sugar

4 egg yolks

4 teaspoons grated lime zest

14-oz. can sweetened condensed milk

½ cup fresh lime juice (from 3-4 large limes, or approximately 15 key limes)

1. Preheat the oven to 325°.
2. Melt the butter. Mix the graham cracker crumbs and sugar in a bowl. Add the butter and stir with a fork.
3. Scrape this mixture into a 9-inch pie pan. Press the crumb mixture into the pie plate to make sure that the mixture forms a firm crust.
4. Bake 10-12 minutes, until the crust is slightly brown.
5. Remove the pie plate from the oven. Let the crust cool to room temperature, about 15 minutes.
6. Whisk the egg yolks and lime zest together in the bowl of a stand mixer until the mixture is tinted light green (about 2 minutes).
7. Beat the sweetened condensed milk into the egg mixture, and then the juice. Set aside at room temperature until it thickens, about 2-3 minutes.
8. Pour the lime mixture into the crust, spread it evenly, and bake for 15 minutes, until the center is set but still wiggles when shaken.
9. Remove the pie from the oven and cool to room temperature.
10. Refrigerate for at least 3 hours until well chilled. Then cut into wedges and serve.

Kids Stuff

My Canadian mother-in-law made
these treats only at Christmas, for good
reason! She made them with the colorful
marshmallows—remember those?

Rich and smooth, these bars
do a quick disappearing act.
A really good "Broad," like
Lynnette, would make her
own marshmallows. But I opt
for the packaged ones.

Butterscotch Marshmallow Slices

KRISTIE ROSSET

Makes 20 small squares

Prep Time: 15 minutes ❧ *Chilling Time: at least one hour*

6 oz. butterscotch morsels/chips (half a typical package)

4 Tablespoons (half a stick) butter

1 cup chunky peanut butter, all-natural peanut butter preferred

2 cups miniature marshmallows

1. Grease an 8 × 8-inch baking pan.
2. In a microwave-safe bowl, melt the butterscotch chips and butter in the microwave for several 10-15-seconds-long intervals to avoid boiling the butter and burning the chips. Stir frequently until the mixture is smooth and lump-free.
3. Stir in the peanut butter until smooth. Add the marshmallows and stir.
4. Spoon into the prepared pan. Refrigerate for at least an hour before slicing and serving.

No-Bake Chocolate Nut Butter Cookies

KRISTIE ROSSET

Makes 36 cookies

Prep Time: 5-10 minutes   *Cooking Time: 10 minutes*

½ heaping cup chunky peanut butter, *or* another type of nut butter

3 cups old-fashioned oats

2 cups sugar

¼ cup unsweetened cocoa powder

½ cup milk

8 Tablespoons (1 stick) butter, cut into chunks

½ teaspoon vanilla extract

1. Prepare two baking sheets or pans by lining them with parchment or wax paper.
2. Measure the peanut butter and oats (without mixing them together) and set them aside. You'll need them to be ready to mix into the dough in just a few minutes.
3. Combine the sugar, cocoa powder, milk, and butter in a saucepan. Bring to a full boil. Then boil for one additional minute, stirring constantly. *Do not overcook beyond one minute*, or the cookies will be crumbly.
4. Remove from the heat and stir in the vanilla, peanut butter, and oats.
5. Drop by spoonfuls onto the prepared cookie sheets.
6. Cool thoroughly before removing and placing on a serving plate. Or eat directly from the parchment paper!

As a child, I loved to make cookies and pie dough. My mother was a thoroughly "modern" woman during the '60s, so TV dinners were our mainstay. But cookies were my domain, and I loved trying any cookie with chocolate.

This recipe was one of my favorites, since the time between making the cookies and eating the cookies was very short! When culling cookbooks recently, I discovered my 1982 Zale Day Care Center Cookbook and this old recipe that I had submitted. On the cover of the cookbook is our eldest daughter as a toddler, and she is now the mother of our grandchildren. Making the cookies brought back all sorts of memories, which is one of the joys of being in the kitchen.

Hello Dollies

ELLEN GUTMAN CHENAUX

Makes 16 servings

Prep Time: 10 minutes ❧ *Baking Time: 30-40 minutes*

5⅓ Tablespoons butter

1 cup graham cracker crumbs

1 cup chocolate chips

1 cup coconut flakes

1 can sweetened condensed milk

1. Preheat the oven to 350°.
2. Melt the butter in an 8- or 9-inch square pan in the oven.
3. Being careful not to burn your fingers, spread the graham cracker crumbs over the melted butter in the bottom of the pan.
4. Then spread the chocolate chips evenly over the top.
5. Then spread the coconut flakes evenly on top.
6. Pour the condensed milk evenly over top.
7. Bake for 30-40 minutes.
8. Let cool. Then cut into 16 squares.

Ooey, gooey delicious! When my son Peter was in third or fourth grade, his class created a cookbook of their favorite foods. Of course, most of the recipes were sweet desserts. This was Peter's contribution.

Graham Cracker Chocolate Chip Cookies

KRISTIE ROSSET

Makes 36 cookies

Prep Time: 10 minutes ❧ *Baking Time: 12 minutes per baking sheet*

5 cups crushed graham crackers

2 cans sweetened condensed milk

12-oz. package milk, *or* semisweet, chocolate chips

1 teaspoon vanilla

½ cup chopped pecans, *optional*

1. Preheat the oven to 350°. Line 3 baking sheets with parchment paper.
2. Place all ingredients in a large mixing bowl and stir thoroughly. The batter will be very thick.
3. Scoop the cookie dough by spoonfuls onto the baking sheets, 12 cookies per sheet.
4. Bake for 10-12 minutes, or until the tops no longer look moist and the edges are lightly golden brown.
5. Remove from the oven. Allow the cookies to rest for a couple of minutes prior to moving them onto wire racks for cooling.

When I was 10, this recipe is the one my best friend and I made whenever we spent the night together. We found it equally good baked or unbaked!

Kids Stuff

Chocolate-Covered Corn Flake Cookies

ELLEN GUTMAN CHENAUX

Makes 2-3 dozen cookies

Prep Time: 10 minutes *Chilling Time: 5 minutes*

4 cups corn flakes

16 oz. bittersweet chocolate, melted, *divided*

1. Put the corn flakes in a large mixing bowl, and pour half of the melted chocolate over them.
2. Mix the corn flakes and chocolate with your fingers (being careful not to crush the cereal) until the corn flakes are evenly coated. The chocolate will begin to set immediately.
3. Add the remaining melted chocolate, mixing the corn flakes and chocolate again.
4. Place parchment paper on a cookie sheet. Using a small ice cream scoop, or two tablespoons, scoop the batter into small mounds on the parchment paper.
5. Refrigerate the cookies for at least 5 minutes to set.
6. You can store the cookies in an airtight container for up to two weeks – if they miraculously last that long!

When my son Peter was 6 or 7, we were having old family friends, well-known restauranteurs from Puerto Rico, for dinner. Peter asked if he could make dessert. Not quite sure how this would go over, I reluctantly agreed. Peter made these cookies, and the friends loved them so much that they asked Peter for his recipe. Perhaps that was the beginning of Peter's culinary career.

Chocolate Cake in a Mug

ELLEN GUTMAN CHENAUX

Makes 1 serving

Prep Time: 2 minutes ❧ *Cooking Time: 3 minutes* ❧ *Cooling Time: 3 minutes*

4 Tablespoons flour

4 Tablespoons sugar

3 Tablespoons unsweetened cocoa powder

1 egg

3 Tablespoons milk

3 Tablespoons vegetable oil

1 Tablespoon chocolate chips

splash of vanilla

1. Place the flour, sugar, and cocoa powder into a good-sized coffee mug. Stir well.
2. Add the egg and mix thoroughly.
3. Pour in the milk and oil and mix well.
4. Add the chocolate chips and vanilla and stir well.
5. Cook for three minutes on high in the microwave. The cake will come to the top of the mug so don't be concerned.
6. Let cool for 3 minutes. Then eat!

This is one of those recipes passed along from friend to friend to friend. The most dangerous thing about this cake is that you are always only five minutes away from chocolate cake at any time of day or night!

Kids Stuff

Kids Stuff

Gourmet Caramel Popcorn

DEBBIE MOSIMANN

Makes about 10 servings

Prep Time: 35 minutes ❧ *Baking Time: 60 minutes* ❧ *Cooling Time: about one hour*

10 cups popped popcorn

1 cup pecan pieces

¾ cup brown sugar, packed

¼ cup light corn syrup

¼ cup maple syrup

8 Tablespoons (1 stick) butter, cut in chunks

⅛ teaspoon cream of tartar

½ teaspoon kosher salt

½ teaspoon baking soda

½ cup white chocolate wafers

½ cup dark chocolate wafers

1. Preheat the oven to 200°. Spray a baking sheet with non-stick cooking spray.
2. Spread the popped popcorn and pecans on the prepared baking sheet. Set aside.
3. Combine the sugar, corn syrup, maple syrup, butter, cream of tartar, and salt in a good-sized saucepan. Stir over medium-high heat just until it boils.
4. Remove from the heat and stir in the baking soda. It will foam like crazy. Immediately pour over the popcorn and toss so that everything is evenly coated.
5. Bake for 1 hour, stirring every 15 minutes.
6. Remove from the oven and allow to cool.
7. When the popcorn is cool, melt the white chocolate over water in a double boiler. Stir with a fork until smooth.
8. In a different bowl, melt the dark chocolate over simmering water. Stir with a fork until smooth.
9. Using a whisk, drizzle the white chocolate over the cooled popcorn. Then drizzle the dark chocolate over the works.
10. Allow to cool and set.
11. Break the popcorn up and store in an airtight container.

So easy to make and so very good. Keep this treat on hand during the holidays for guests to munch on, or to give as gifts.

Grandpa's Popcorn Balls

KRISTIE ROSSET

Makes 12 servings

Prep Time: 10 minutes *Cooking Time: 15 minutes*

5 quarts popped popcorn
(not microwaved)

2 cups sugar

½ cup white corn syrup

½ cup water

1. Place the popped corn in a very large bowl, allowing room for stirring.
2. In a heavy saucepan, cook the sugar, syrup, and water over medium-high heat to a firm ball stage, using the cold-water method: Drop ½-1 teaspoon of the syrup you've just been cooking into a small bowl of very cold water. If that drop creates a firm ball, the syrup is finished.
3. Remove from the heat and pour over the popcorn. Stir gently with a spatula or wooden spoon.
4. Thoroughly grease your hands with butter and mold the popcorn into balls. Note: the syrup is very hot so be careful! Also, bigger hands = bigger popcorn balls.

The kids always wanted the popcorn balls that Grandpa molded—they were the largest and tastiest.

Kids Stuff

Puppy Chow

YVONNE MARTIN

Prep time: 10 minutes

Makes 8-9 cups of snack cereal

8-9 cups Chex cereal—corn, *or* rice, *or* a mixture

4 Tablespoons (half a stick) butter

1 cup chocolate chips

½ cup, or more, peanut butter

confectioners sugar to coat, about 1-1½ cups

1. Measure the cereal into a large bowl. If you have a really big plastic bowl with a lid, it makes the last step of the recipe easier. If not, use a Ziploc bag instead.
2. Place the butter, chocolate chips, and peanut butter together in a microwave-safe bowl. Microwave on high in 15-second increments, stirring after every 15 seconds.
3. Pour the melted chocolate mixture over the cereal and stir gently to coat.
4. Allow to cool slightly.
5. If you have a large bowl with a lid, sprinkle a cup of the powdered sugar over the cereal, put on the lid, and shake it gently to coat all the pieces. If you're using a Ziploc bag, transfer half the coated cereal mixture to the bag and add half the confectioners sugar. Seal and shake the bag, emptying the bag before adding the rest of the cereal and sugar. Repeat with the remaining cereal and sugar. You may need more sugar to fully coat the cereal.
6. Spread the coated cereal on waxed paper to cool.
7. Store in a tightly covered container in a cool place.

It's impossible to make this without getting your hands covered in chocolate and confectioners sugar, but it's fun to lick the mess off when you're done! This recipe is also known by other names like Muddy Buddies, Reindeer Chow, or Monkey Munch. This recipe never makes enough!

Chocolate Mousse Surprise (VEGAN)

KRISTIE ROSSET

Serves: 8

Prep Time: 15 minutes ✀ *Chilling Time: 3 hours or more*

4 soft avocados

¾ cup unsweetened cocoa powder

½ cup agave nectar

½ cup Stevia (the powder that equals sugar in measurement), *or* sugar

optional toppings: fresh berries, crushed peppermint candies, grated coconut, slivered or chopped nuts, dessert sauces, or whipped cream, and more

1. Place avocado meat in the bowl of a large food processor. Add the cocoa powder, agave nectar, and Stevia. Process until smooth, scraping the bowl occasionally.
2. Spoon into small dessert bowls and chill for a minimum of 3 hours.
3. If you wish, top with any or several of these: fresh raspberries *or* strawberries, crushed peppermint candy, grated coconut, slivered almonds *or* pecans, butterscotch *or* caramel sauce, *or* whipped cream. The variety is endless.

I overheard a friend describing a delicious, dairy-free chocolate mousse that she had tasted, with the base made from avocados. The image in my head was not a pretty one, and I simply could not imagine mixing chocolate with avocado. So with a little experimenting comes this simple, delicious, and rich chocolate mousse. Since many folks, like me, manage Type II diabetes, I've used Stevia to enhance the sweetness. This dessert is the perfect non-dairy, low-carb, divine sweetness that I crave. Even my granddaughter, who cannot tolerate dairy but loves avocados, can make this dessert.

Oreo Snowballs

KRISTIE ROSSET

Makes 3 dozen "snowballs"

Prep Time: 60 minutes *Chilling Time: 1 hour*

35 regular Oreo cookies

6 oz. cream cheese, cut into chunks and softened to room temperature

12- *or* 16-oz. package white chocolate almond bark, *or* morsels

2 cups coconut flakes

1. Prepare baking sheets by lining them with parchment paper.
2. Place the Oreos and cream cheese in a large food processor bowl. Process until the cookies are fine crumbs and the mixture clings together, forming a ball.
3. Remove the dough from the processor. Pull off pieces of the dough and roll them into balls, approximately 1½ inches in diameter.
4. Chill the balls in the refrigerator for at least an hour.
5. Meanwhile, melt the white chocolate in the microwave on high, stirring every 30 seconds until smooth.
6. Taking a few balls out of the refrigerator at a time, roll each in the white chocolate and place on the baking sheets. Allow the balls to sit for a moment, so that the white chocolate sets partially, yet is still sticky.
7. Roll the balls in the coconut. Allow to cool.
8. Store the snowballs in a sealed container in the refrigerator.

A chocolate snowball hiding inside! Kids and adults love these fun cookies, especially in the wintertime. Share the dough-rolling with youngsters.

Easy as Pi, 3.14

Apple Crumb Pie

JOYCE SCHULTE

Makes one 9-inch pie, 8 servings

Prep Time: 45 minutes ✀ *Baking Time: 50-60 minutes*

pastry dough for a single crust 9-inch pie (recipe on pages 200-201, or your own favorite)

4 large, tart apples (Granny Smith works well)

1 cup sugar, *divided*

1 teaspoon cinnamon

½ cup sugar

¾ cup enriched flour

5⅓ Tablespoons cold butter

1. Preheat the oven to 400°.
2. Peel and core the apples. Cut each apple into eight slices and arrange in a pastry-lined 9-inch pie pan.
3. Mix ½ cup sugar with cinnamon. Sprinkle evenly over the apples.
4. Sift the remaining ½ cup sugar with the flour.
5. Cut in the butter until the mixture is crumbly.
6. Sprinkle over the apples.
7. Bake in the oven for 50-60 minutes, until the apples are tender and the pie is browned.

My husband is from Michigan, and Michigan is known for its apples. My mother-in-law is known for her pies so put the two together. This pie was a regular at the Thanksgiving and Christmas tables while my husband was growing up. I like the crumble as a topping instead of the traditional lattice top crust. This recipe is a little sweeter than some, and it goes really well with vanilla ice cream!

Lemon Shaker Pie

JOYCE SCHULTE

Makes 1 9-inch pie, 8 servings

Prep Time: 30 minutes ❧ *Standing Time: at least 4 hours* ❧ *Baking Time: 35 minutes*

1 baked 9-inch
pie shell, plus
unbaked pastry
for the top crust

2 large lemons,
sliced paper thin

2 cups sugar

4 eggs, well
beaten

1. Slice the lemons as thin as paper, rind and all. Seriously, make them thin. A mandolin makes thin, evenly sized slices.
2. Combine the sliced lemons with the sugar and mix well.
3. Let stand at least 4 hours or longer, mixing together occasionally if possible. You can also let them stand overnight, which makes the pie a little less tart.
4. Preheat the oven to 450°.
5. Add the beaten eggs to the lemon mixture and mix well.
6. Turn the filling into the baked pie shell, arranging the lemon slices evenly.
7. Cover with a top crust. Cut several slits near the center.
8. Bake for 15 minutes.
9. Then reduce the heat to 375° and bake for an additional 20 minutes or until a knife inserted near the edge of the pie comes out clean.
10. Cool completely before serving.

This is a classic recipe in the Shaker tradition, and my husband loves it! His mother has been making it ever since their family first tasted it on a visit to Shakertown in Wilmore, Kentucky, years ago. This is a very tart lemon pie, using whole lemons, rind, and all. Slice 'em thin, let 'em stand in the sugar mixture for the full 4 hours, and then pucker up. Because if you love lemons, you are absolutely gonna love this pie!

Apple Walnut Pie

KATHRYN WHITE

Makes one 9-inch pie, 8 servings

Prep Time: 30 minutes *Baking Time: 60 minutes total*

1 cup flour

3 oz. cream cheese, softened to room temperature

8 Tablespoons (1 stick) butter, softened to room temperature

⅓ cup flour

½ teaspoon cinnamon

½ teaspoon freshly grated nutmeg

¼ teaspoon salt

1⅔ cups sour cream

1 cup sugar

1 large egg, lightly beaten

2 teaspoons vanilla

6 large apples (Granny Smith, *or* your favorite), peeled, cored, and sliced

1 cup chopped walnuts

1. Preheat the oven to 450°.
2. Make the dough for the crust by combining 1 cup flour, cream cheese, and 8 Tablespoons butter with a pastry cutter. Be sure the ingredients are well blended.
3. Press the dough into a 9-inch pie plate.
4. Place ⅓ cup flour, cinnamon, nutmeg, and ¼ teaspoon salt in a small bowl. Whisk to combine.
5. In a large bowl, combine the sour cream, sugar, egg, and vanilla.
6. Stir the flour mixture into the sour cream mixture, whisking the ingredients until well combined.
7. Add the apples. Use a large spoon to blend everything together.
8. Pour the apple mixture over the crust in the pie plate.
9. Bake for 10 minutes at 450°. Then reduce the heat to 350° and bake for 35 minutes.
10. While the pie is in the oven, combine the chopped walnuts, ½ cup flour, 8 Tablespoons butter, brown sugar, maple syrup, cinnamon, and ¼ teaspoon salt. Use a spoon or spatula to blend the ingredients well in a medium bowl.

½ cup flour

8 Tablespoons (1 stick) butter, softened to room temperature

⅓ cup brown sugar

3 Tablespoons maple syrup

2 teaspoons cinnamon

¼ teaspoon salt

11. Remove the pie from the oven and spoon the topping over the apples. Return the pie to the oven and bake another 15 minutes.
12. Let finished pie cool at least 15 minutes before slicing.
13. Serve with vanilla ice cream if you wish.

This is a favorite of mine. The sour cream is an unexpected surprise, and the topping is a perfect match of walnuts and brown sugar.

While this pie is best made with fresh rhubarb, it can also be made with frozen. I love the tartness of rhubarb, and this is a favorite pie in our house, even though we don't grow rhubarb.

Easy as Pi, 3.14

Rhubarb Pie

JOYCE SCHULTE

Makes one 9-inch pie, 8 servings
Prep Time: 20 minutes   Baking Time: 45 minutes

3 Tablespoons flour

1 cup sugar

1 egg, beaten

2 cups fresh, *or* thawed frozen, rhubarb (drain well if using thawed), cut into ¼-inch-thick slices

pastry dough for two pie crusts (see recipe on pages 200-201)

1. Preheat the oven to 425°.
2. Sift the flour and sugar together into a good-sized bowl.
3. Add the egg and beat thoroughly.
4. Stir in the rhubarb.
5. Pour the filling into the unbaked 9-inch pie shell.
6. Cover with a top crust or lattice crust.
7. Bake for 10 minutes.
8. Reduce the heat to 350° and bake 35 minutes longer.
9. Allow to cool to warm or room temperature before cutting to serve.

My mother-in-law, like any good Midwesterner, had a backyard garden. Rhubarb was one of the staples in that garden, and my husband remembers eating a lot of rhubarb pie while growing up.

Can She Bake a Blueberry Pie?

ELLEN GUTMAN CHENAUX

Makes one 9-inch pie, 8 servings

Prep Time: 15-20 minutes ❧ Standing Time: 30 minutes ❧ Freezing Time: 10 minutes
Baking Time: 40-50 minutes, or a bit more if you use a deep dish pie plate
Cooling time: 3-4 hours

pastry dough for a double-crust pie (see recipe on pages 200-201, or your own favorite)

4 pints fresh blueberries

5 tablespoons cornstarch, flour, *or* quick-cooking tapioca

1 teaspoon lemon zest, finely grated

2 Tablespoons fresh lemon juice

¼ teaspoon salt

¾ cup sugar, plus a bit more for the top of the pie

1 large egg

1. Roll out half of the pie dough into a 10-inch round. Carefully place in a 9-inch pie plate. Trim the dough leaving a ½-inch overhang.
2. Toss the berries, cornstarch, lemon zest, lemon juice, salt, and sugar in a large mixing bowl. Let the mixture stand for 30 minutes.
3. Preheat the oven to 425°.
4. Pour the filling into the pie shell.
5. Roll out the second pastry disk into a 10-inch round. Place the pastry on top of the filling.
6. Crimp the top and bottom edges together to seal.
7. Score the top pastry with several cuts to vent the filling. Or cut the dough into strips to cover the pie with lattice work. Place and weave the strips on top of the filling, leaving a ½-inch overhang. Crimp the top and bottom pastry edges together to seal.
8. Beat the egg. Brush the top pastry and edges. Sprinkle with extra sugar.
9. Place the pie in the freezer for 10 minutes.

She sure can, and so can you! Everybody loves blueberry pie. Just ask any diner. And blueberries are a superfood—neutralizing free radicals, protecting the heart, improving vision, and helping protect against degenerative brain disease!

10. Cover the pie edges with foil or a pie crust shield to prevent the edges from over-browning.
11. Place the pie in the oven. Place a baking sheet on the rack below the pie.
12. Bake 10 minutes at 425°. Then reduce the oven temperature to 375°. Continue baking for 30-40 minutes (longer if using a deep-dish pie plate).
13. Tent the pie with foil if it seems to be cooking too quickly. Remove the foil or pie crust shield about 10 minutes before removing the pie from the oven.
14. Continue baking until the crust is a golden brown and the filling is bubbling.
15. Transfer the pie to a wire rack. Let the pie cool for 3-4 hours before serving to allow the filling to set.

Lemon Sponge Pie

DEBBIE MOSIMANN

Makes one 9-inch pie, 8 servings

Prep Time: 20 minutes if the pie crust is already made; 30 minutes if you're making the pie crust from scratch ❧ *Baking Time: 40-45 minutes*

1 9-inch pie shell (see recipe on pages 200-201)

5⅓ Tablespoons butter, softened to room temperature

1 cup sugar

2 eggs

3 lemons, from which you'll need 3 teaspoons lemon zest (and juice below)

¾ cup fresh lemon juice

2 Tablespoons flour

¼ teaspoon salt

1 cup milk

1. Preheat the oven to 450°.
2. Prepare the pastry and place it in a 9-inch pie pan. Line it with aluminum foil. Bake the crust for 5 minutes to allow it to set.
3. Remove the foil and bake another 5 minutes. Remove the pie shell from the oven. Cool to room temperature.
4. In a large bowl beat the butter until light and smooth. Add the sugar and beat for 1 minute.
5. Separate the eggs, reserving both the yolks and the whites. Add the yolks one at a time to the creamed mixture. Beat well after each addition until light and fluffy.
6. Add the lemon zest, juice, flour, and salt. Slowly add the milk and mix until just combined.
7. In a separate bowl with clean beaters, beat the egg whites until they form stiff peaks.
8. Fold the egg whites into the egg yolk mixture and pour into the prepared pie shell.
9. Reduce the oven temperature to 400°. Bake the pie for 30-35 minutes, or until the filling is set and a knife inserted into the center comes out clean.
10. Cool. Then refrigerate or freeze until time to serve.

Easy as Pi, 3.14

Chocolate Cream Pie

JOYCE SCHULTE

Makes one 9-inch pie, 8 servings

Prep Time: 15 minutes ❧ *Cooling Time: 30 minutes* ❧ *Baking Time: 15-20 minutes*

pastry dough for a single crust 9-inch pie (recipe on pages 200-201, or your own favorite), baked

2 squares unsweetened baking chocolate (2-3 oz.), broken up into small pieces

⅔ cup sugar

⅓ cup flour

⅛ teaspoon salt

2 cups milk

3 egg yolks

1 teaspoon vanilla

3 egg whites

6 Tablespoons sugar, *divided*

1. Combine the chocolate, sugar, flour, and salt in a saucepan.
2. Add the milk and egg yolks.
3. Cook over low heat, stirring constantly until the filling becomes creamy and thickens. Cook the filling until it is very thick and looks like a pie filling or a pudding. Note: it will not get much thicker when you bake the pie.
4. Add the vanilla and let cool about 30 minutes.
5. Preheat the oven to 350°.
6. Meanwhile, make the meringue. Beat the egg whites to soft peaks.
7. Stir in the sugar, 1 Tablespoon at a time, and beat the mixture until stiff peaks form.
8. Pour the cooled chocolate filling into the baked pie shell.
9. Add the meringue on top, covering the chocolate all the way to the edges.
10. Bake for about 15-20 minutes, or until the meringue is nicely browned.

My grandma made this pie for me every summer when we went to Indiana. She always said it was her favorite. It sure was mine!

Peaches and Cream Pie

DEBBIE MOSIMANN

Makes one 8-inch, deep-dish pie, 8 servings

Prep Time: 30 minutes ❧ *Baking Time: 35 minutes* ❧ *Chilling Time: 2-8 hours*

½ cup graham cracker crumbs

½ cup almond flour

⅓ cup sugar

⅛ teaspoon salt

4 Tablespoons (half a stick) melted butter

12 ozs. cream cheese, softened to room temperature

2 large eggs, *divided*

⅓ cup sugar

¼ cup sour cream

1 lemon, juice and zest

1 Tablespoon cornstarch

¼ cup water

3 Tablespoons cornstarch

2 cups orange juice

½ cup sugar

2 cups peeled peach slices

½ cup mashed peaches

1. Preheat the oven to 350°.
2. In a bowl combine the graham cracker crumbs, almond flour, ⅓ cup sugar, salt, and melted butter until damp. Then press into an 8-inch, deep pie dish, covering the bottom and up the sides in an even thickness.
3. Bake for 10 minutes. Remove from the oven and cool to room temperature. Reduce the oven temperature to 325°.
4. In a mixing bowl and using a hand mixer, beat the cream cheese until soft and creamy.
5. Add the eggs one at a time, mixing well.
6. Mix in ⅓ cup sugar. Then add the sour cream, lemon juice, lemon zest, and 1 Tablespoon cornstarch. Beat until smooth.
7. Pour into the cooled graham cracker crust.
8. Bake at 325° for 25 minutes, or until a knife inserted into the center comes out clean.
9. Remove from the oven. Allow to cool to room temperature.
10. In a large saucepan, whisk the water, 3 Tablespoons cornstarch, and orange juice together. Whisk in the ½ cup sugar.
11. Bring the mixture to a boil, stirring constantly until thickened. Remove from the heat.

12. Prepare the peaches, slicing the 2 cups and mashing the ½ cup.
13. Add the mashed peaches to the orange juice mixture and stir.
14. Add the sliced peaches and stir.
15. Pour over the baked, cooled cheesecake pie.
16. Refrigerate until set, at least 1 hour, but better yet, overnight.

A cross between a peach pie and a cheesecake, this is a great way to use fresh peaches.

Bourbon Ginger Pecan Pie

ELLEN GUTMAN CHENAUX

Makes one 9-inch pie, 8 servings

Prep Time: 25 minutes for the filling ✖ *Pecan Roasting Time: 8-10 minutes*
Baking Time: 40-50 minutes

pastry dough for a single crust 9-inch pie (recipe on pages 200-201, or your own favorite)

1¼ cups pecan halves, lightly roasted

3 eggs, lightly beaten

1 cup sugar

½ cup light corn syrup

½ cup dark corn syrup

5⅓ Tablespoons butter, unsalted, melted and cooled

2 Tablespoons bourbon

1 teaspoon ground ginger

1 teaspoon vanilla

¼ teaspoon salt

¼ cup diced fresh ginger, *optional*

whipped cream

1. Place the dough into the bottom of a 9-inch pie plate.
2. Preheat the oven to 350°.
3. Spread the pecans on a baking sheet in a single layer. Roast them for 8-10 minutes, or until they're lightly browned. Cool.
4. Turn the oven up to 375°.
5. In a good-sized bowl, mix together the eggs, sugar, corn syrups, butter, bourbon, ground ginger, vanilla, and salt until well blended.
6. Sprinkle the bottom of the pie shell with the pecans and diced fresh ginger if you wish.
7. Pour the egg mixture on top of the pecans and ginger.
8. Place the pie on the middle rack of the oven with a baking sheet on the bottom rack under the pie.

9. Bake, protecting the crust edges with either a pie saver or foil, for 40-50 minutes, until just set at the edges but still somewhat loose in the center.
10. Place on a wire rack to cool.
11. Serve with a dollop of whipped cream on each slice.

Don't wait for a holiday to try this recipe. The bourbon and ginger make this pecan pie soar!

Frangelica Chocolate Silk Pie

KRISTIE ROSSET

Makes 12 servings

Prep Time: 1 hour ❧ *Chilling Time: 3-8 hours, or overnight*

1 cup graham cracker crumbs

3 Tablespoons butter, melted

7 oz. semisweet chocolate

16 Tablespoons (2 sticks) butter, softened

½ cup sugar

4 eggs, *divided*

1 teaspoon vanilla

2 Tablespoons brandy

2 Tablespoons Frangelica liqueur

1½ cups heavy cream

¼ cup sugar

1 Tablespoon unsweetened cocoa powder

½ Tablespoon unflavored gelatin

¼ cup water

shaved chocolate for garnish

1. Mix together the graham crumbs and 3 Tablespoons butter. Press the mixture into the bottom of a 10-inch springform pan.
2. For the filling, melt the chocolate in the microwave in 15-second intervals on high. Stir after each interval, just until the chocolate is melted.
3. In a stand mixer, beat together the 16 Tablespoons butter and ½ cup sugar. Add the melted chocolate. Beat on low until incorporated.
4. Beat in the eggs, one at a time.
5. Stir in the vanilla, brandy, and Frangelica until mixed in thoroughly.
6. Pour the filling into the crust.
7. Whip the heavy cream in a stand mixer. As the cream begins to thicken, fold in the ¼ cup of sugar by tablespoonsful. Continue whipping until soft peaks form.
8. In a small bowl, mix together the cocoa powder, gelatin, and water. Allow to stand until the gelatin is dissolved. Microwave for 15 seconds and stir. Repeat until the gelatin is totally dissolved.
9. Gently add the cocoa mixture to the whipped cream. Beat on low to incorporate.
10. Spread over the filling.
11. Refrigerate for 3-8 hours, until set.
12. Top with shaved chocolate to serve.

The smoothest chocolate pie you'll ever eat! This pie found me on a visit to Vancouver, Canada, for the 1988 World Expo. The restaurant is long since closed, but the recipe lives on. It's a true family favorite, and it impresses guests.

Raspberry Cheesecake Pie

YVONNE MARTIN

Makes 2 9-inch pies, 16-20 servings

Prep Time: 20 minutes ❧ *Chilling Time: 2-8 hours*

3 cups graham cracker crumbs

½ cup sugar

10⅔ Tablespoons (⅔ cup) melted butter

2 Tablespoons hot water

1 envelope unflavored gelatin

2 8-oz. packages cream cheese, softened to room temperature

14-oz. can sweetened condensed milk

⅓ cup lemon juice

1 teaspoon vanilla extract

6-oz. package raspberry gelatin

2 cups boiling water

32-oz. package frozen raspberries

whipped cream and fresh mint leaves

1. Combine the cracker crumbs, sugar, and melted butter.
2. Press into bottom of two ungreased 9-inch pie plates or two 8-inch springform pans. Put the plates or pans in the freezer to chill while you make the filling.
3. Pour 2 Tablespoons hot water into a small bowl. Sprinkle the envelope of unflavored gelatin over top. Stir until it dissolves and then set aside.
4. Beat the cream cheese and sweetened condensed milk together. Stir in the gelatin mixture, lemon juice, and vanilla.
5. Divide this mixture evenly between the two pie plates or springform pans and smooth the tops. Refrigerate.
6. Dissolve the raspberry gelatin in the boiling water. Stir in the frozen raspberries. Spoon gently over the filling in the two pans.
7. Refrigerate for at least 2 hours, preferably overnight. Cut into wedges to serve.
8. Garnish with whipped cream and mint.

This is the perfect dessert for a hot summer day. You don't have to turn on the stove or oven, and the finished product is light, fruity and cool.

Buttermilk Pie

KATHRYN WHITE

Makes 6-8 servings

Prep Time: 15 minutes ❧ *Baking Time: 55 minutes*

pastry dough for a single crust
9-inch pie (recipe on pages
200-201, or your own favorite)

3 Tablespoons flour

1¼ cups sugar

4 large eggs, slightly beaten

4 Tablespoons (half a
stick) butter, melted

1 cup buttermilk

zest of 1 lemon

1 Tablespoon fresh lemon juice

1 teaspoon vanilla extract

2 teaspoons freshly
grated nutmeg

1. Place the pastry dough into the pie plate.
2. Preheat the oven to 425°.
3. Combine the flour and sugar in a medium bowl and whisk to blend.
4. Add the beaten eggs and, using an electric hand mixer, mix well.
5. Stir in the butter and buttermilk.
6. Add the lemon zest, lemon juice, vanilla, and nutmeg. Mix on low until blended.
7. Pour the mixture into the unbaked pie shell.
8. Place the pie in the center of the oven and bake at 425° for 15 minutes.
9. Lower the temperature to 350° and bake for another 40 minutes or until the filling is set. It will be light golden brown in color.
10. Cool to room temperature and serve.
11. The pie will keep in the refrigerator; bring to room temperature to serve.

I first ate a slice of buttermilk pie in Springfield, Missouri, while visiting family. Then I had a second piece. Just sayin'...

Pies in a Jar

DEBBIE MOSIMANN

Makes 8 servings

Prep Time: 35 minutes *Baking Time: 30 -40 minutes, or until the tops are golden brown*

8 half-pint, squat, wide-mouth, 1-cup Mason jars

pastry for one 9-inch pie (see recipe on pages 200-201, or use your own recipe)

4½ cups fruit (strawberries, rhubarb, *or* blueberries, *or* a fruit combination)

¾ cup sugar

6 Tablespoons cornstarch

1 Tablespoon lemon juice

1 egg

1 Tablespoon water

1 Tablespoon coarse sanding sugar for the tops, *optional*

1. Preheat the oven to 400°.
2. Roll out the pastry and cut into ½-inch-wide strips.
3. In a good-sized bowl, toss the berries with the ¾ cup sugar, cornstarch, and lemon juice.
4. Fill the jars heaping full with the berry mixture.
5. Basket-weave the strips of dough across the top of the fruit. Pinch around the edges and place on a baking sheet.
6. Whisk the egg with the water and paint the tops of the lattice pie dough.
7. If you wish, sprinkle the top with coarse sanding sugar.
8. Bake until the tops turn brown and the filling bubbles, about 30 -40 minutes.
9. Remove from the oven and cool.

Easy as pie! And lots of fun!

Easy as Pi, 3.14

Pastry Dough

ELLEN GUTMAN CHENAUX

Makes two pie crusts, or one double-crust

Prep Time: 10-15 minutes ✎ *Chilling Time: 60 minutes or more*

Among us, I am known as the Pie Broad. My grandmother taught me to make pie crust when I was too young to know that pastry intimidates many bakers. Fear not! The food processor makes pie baking easy as... well, pie!

2 cups flour, plus more
for the rolling process

⅔ teaspoon salt

16 Tablespoons
(2 sticks) unsalted
butter, very cold
and cut into cubes

2 cold egg yolks

ice water

1. Place the flour and salt into the bowl of a food processor fitted with a steel blade. Process for a second or two to mix.
2. Drop the cold butter into the feed chute of the food processor. Process until the butter is incorporated, about 15 seconds, and the mixture resembles coarse meal.
3. In a 1-cup liquid measuring cup, lightly beat the yolks with a fork. Add enough ice water to the egg yolks to yield ½ cup liquid.
4. Start the food processor and slowly add the egg/ ice water mixture through the feed chute into the flour/butter mixture in a steady stream.
5. When the dough *just begins* to form a ball, in about 6 seconds, stop the processor. (You may need to add a few more drops of ice water for this to happen.) Be careful not to over-process.
6. Transfer the dough to a lightly floured pastry mat or, even better, a marble slab. The colder the mat or board, the better.
7. Knead the dough for a couple of minutes until the butter is mostly incorporated, about 4-8 kneads. Then cut the ball in half, creating two balls. Flatten each ball into a disk.
8. Wrap each disk in wax paper and cover with plastic wrap.
9. Refrigerate for an hour or more. Or place the wrapped disks in a freezer bag and store in the freezer for up to two months.

Pastry Cream

ELLEN GUTMAN CHENAUX

Makes 2½ cups

Prep Time: 15-20 minutes ❧ *Cooking Time: 20 minutes*
Cooling Time: 30 minutes or more

6 extra-large egg yolks
at room temperature

¾ cup sugar

3 Tablespoons cornstarch

2 cups whole milk

1 vanilla bean, *or*
1 teaspoon vanilla
(a bean gives a fuller
vanilla flavor)

2 Tablespoons (¼ stick)
unsalted butter,
cut into pieces

2 Tablespoons
heavy cream

1 teaspoon Cognac,
or brandy, *optional*

1. In the bowl of a stand mixer, use the paddle attachment to beat the egg yolks and sugar on medium-high for 3 minutes. The mixture should be light yellow and should fall back into the bowl in a ribbon.
2. On low speed, beat in the cornstarch.
3. Bring the milk and vanilla bean (if you're using vanilla extract, you'll add it later) to a boil in a saucepan over medium heat.
4. Turn the mixer on low and slowly pour the milk into the egg mixture.
5. When well mixed, pour the mixture back into the saucepan.
6. Cook over medium heat, stirring constantly with a whisk or wooden spoon until the mixture is thick, about 10 minutes.
7. Bring the mixture to a boil. Then cook on low heat 2-3 minutes. Taste to be sure the cornstarch is cooked.
8. Remove the saucepan from the heat. Remove the vanilla bean. Mix in the butter, cream, Cognac, and vanilla if you are using the extract instead of the bean.
9. Strain the mixture into a bowl. Place plastic wrap directly on the cream and refrigerate until cold.

Lots of recipes call for pastry cream. This one is my favorite!

Proof Is In the Pudding

Baked Egg Custard

DEBBIE MOSIMANN

Makes 12 servings

Prep Time: 30 minutes ✒ *Baking Time: 20 minutes* ✒ *Chilling Time: 8 hours, or overnight*

12 4-oz. ramekins or custard cups

4 large eggs

scant ½ cup sugar

4 cups whole milk

2 Tablespoons vanilla

1 whole nutmeg

1. Preheat the oven to 325°.
2. Whisk the eggs for about 30 seconds in a big bowl.
3. Add the sugar. Whisk another 30 seconds or until the sugar dissolves.
4. Add the milk. Whisk until all ingredients are well combined.
5. Whisk in the vanilla.
6. Place the ramekins in a baking pan whose sides are at least 2 inches high.
7. Pour the egg mixture into the ramekins, filling each to the top.
8. With a microplane or fine grater, grate the whole nutmeg over the egg mixture in each ramekin until the tops are covered. (If you use ground nutmeg, sprinkle on liberally until all the tops are covered.)
9. Place the baking pan in the preheated oven. From the side, fill the pan with hot water until it reaches about halfway up the ramekins.
10. Bake for 20 minutes, or just until a knife inserted into the middle of the egg mixture in the various ramekins comes out clean. Do not overbake.
11. Remove the pan from the oven and allow the water to cool. Remove the ramekins from the water bath and chill overnight.
12. Serve with fresh fruit or berries alongside the custard.

Proof Is In the Pudding

Baked Egg Custard goes back as far as my memory does. It is one of those comfort foods of childhood, though I have realized as an adult that it is really a Lancaster County, PA, dish. It is creamy and delicious. Just be careful not to overbake it.

Blueberry Bread Pudding with Maple Variation

DEBBIE MOSIMANN AND KRISTIE ROSSET

Makes 6 servings

Prep Time: 15 minutes ❧ *Soaking Time: 2-8 hours, or overnight* ❧ *Baking Time: 45 minutes*

1½ cups blueberries, fresh *or* frozen

2 Tablespoons orange liqueur

8 slices, *or* 3 cups cubed, day-old white bread in bite-size pieces, *divided*

8-oz. package cream cheese, cut into ½-inch cubes, *divided*

1½ cups milk

8 eggs

¼ cup honey

1 teaspoon orange zest, *or* orange extract

4 Tablespoons (half a stick) butter, melted

more blueberries, fresh *or* frozen, for topping

whipped cream

1. Toss the berries in a bowl with the liqueur.
2. Butter a 9 × 9-inch baking dish.
3. Place half the cubed bread and half the blueberries in the bottom of the dish.
4. Distribute half the cubed cream cheese over top.
5. Repeat the 3 layers, using all of the bread, blueberries, and cream cheese.
6. In a good-sized bowl, mix together the milk, eggs, honey, and orange zest or extract.
7. Pour over the bread mixture. Cover. Refrigerate for at least two hours, or overnight.
8. Remove from the refrigerator half an hour before baking. Drizzle with the melted butter.
9. Preheat the oven to 350°.
10. Cover the bread pudding with foil. Bake 30 minutes.
11. Remove the foil. Bake an additional 15 minutes, or until a knife inserted into the center comes out clean.
12. Cut into squares. Serve with more fresh blueberries and whipped cream.

Variation:

Maple Pecan Bread Pudding

1. Prepare a 9 × 13-inch baking dish
2. Increase amount of bread to 1 loaf brioche or egg bread, cubed into bite-size pieces.
3. Omit the orange liqueur, blueberries, and orange extract.
4. Replace the milk with 1 quart of whipping cream + 1 cup of maple syrup.
5. Replace the orange extract with 1 Tablespoon vanilla extract.
6. Add 1 cup chopped pecans.
7. Follow the directions above, making the substitutions. Fold the pecans into the batter and sprinkle the top with more pecans before baking. Drizzle with maple syrup before serving.

This is a great way to use stale bread. It's a make-ahead dessert that only needs to be baked the day you serve it.

Instant Pot Rice Pudding with Sautéed Apples

YVONNE MARTIN

Makes 8 servings

Prep Time: 5 minutes ❧ *Cooking Time: 30 minutes (this allows time for the pot to pressurize)*

1 cup Arborio rice

1½ cups water

¼ teaspoon salt

2 cups whole milk

¼ cup sugar

2 eggs

½ cup half-and-half

½ teaspoon vanilla

1 teaspoon cinnamon

¾ cup raisins, *optional*

1. Combine the rice, water, and salt in the Instant Pot. Lock its lid and choose high pressure, 3 minutes. Do a natural pressure release of 10 minutes.
2. Remove the lid and stir the milk and sugar into the rice.
3. Beat the eggs with the half-and-half, vanilla, and cinnamon. Mix into the rice mixture.
4. Set the Instant Pot to sauté and cook, stirring constantly, until it starts to simmer. Then turn off the pot. If you are using raisins, add them now.
5. Serve hot or cold. The mixture will thicken as it cools.

I remember my grandmother and mother making delicious rice puddings, but it seemed to take hours in the oven, with frequent stirring, checking, and adding of more liquid. So when I found this recipe, I couldn't believe it. Rich and creamy rice pudding, ready to eat in about 45 minutes, with only 5 minutes spent stirring and mixing. If you don't have an Instant Pot, this recipe can be made on the stove-top. But you'll have to cook the rice for about 25 minutes before adding the milk, sugar, and eggs.

Proof Is In the Pudding

Sautéed Apple Topping

JOYCE SCHULTE

Makes 8 servings

Prep Time: 15 minutes ✿ *Cooking Time: 20 minutes*

2 Tablespoons (¼ stick) unsalted butter

6 Tablespoons sugar

1 teaspoon ground cinnamon

3 large Granny Smith apples (or any tart, firm, baking apple), peeled, halved, cored, and thinly sliced

1. Melt butter in a wide skillet or sauté pan over low heat. Do not use a deep pan.
2. As the butter is melting, add the sugar and cinnamon, mixing well. Keep the heat low so the glaze doesn't burn.
3. Add sliced apples and stir well.
4. Sauté until the apple slices are tender and golden brown.
5. Pass as a topping for the rice pudding.

Proof Is In the Pudding

Pot de Crème S'mores

DEBBIE MOSIMANN

Makes 8 servings

Prep Time: 15-20 minutes ❧ *Baking Time: 30-35 minutes*
Chilling Time: more than 2 hours

Who doesn't enjoy S'mores by the open fire? These beautiful
rich desserts are just the thing to recreate that memory.

8 4-oz. ramekins
or custard cups

6 ounces good
chocolate, broken
into pieces

1⅓ cups heavy cream

½ cup whole milk

¼ cup strong
coffee, cooled

1 teaspoon
vanilla extract

6 egg yolks (save the
whites for other uses,
such as the Raspberry
Meringue Cake, recipe
on pages 56-57)

2 Tablespoons sugar

8 marshmallows,
homemade, *or*
store-bought

8 graham cracker
quarters

1. Preheat the oven to 300°.
2. Put the chocolate pieces in a heat-proof bowl.
3. In a saucepan, scald the cream, milk, and coffee together.
4. Remove from the heat and pour over the chocolate pieces.
5. Add the vanilla and allow to stand for 1 minute before whisking until smooth.
6. In a separate bowl whisk the egg yolks and sugar until light yellow.
7. Pour the melted chocolate into the egg yolks and whisk until smooth. Cool this mixture to room temperature, stirring regularly.
8. Place a kitchen towel on the bottom of a large baking dish. Place eight 4-ounce ramekins on the towel.
9. Fill the ramekins with the chocolate custard. Place in the oven, and then carefully pour hot water into the pan so that it comes halfway up the sides of the ramekins.
10. Cover with foil. Bake for 30-35 minutes. The Pot de Crème S'mores are done when they're set around the edges and still a little shaky in the middle.
11. Carefully remove from the water bath and transfer to a rack to cool. Cover. When they've reached room temperature, chill for 2-4 hours.
12. When ready to serve, place a marshmallow (to make your own, see recipe on pages 68-69) in the center of each filled ramekin. Brown with a torch or under the broiler.
13. Garnish with a quarter-graham cracker poked into each of the Pots de Crème.

Vanilla Bean Panna Cotta with Blood Orange Gelée

DEBBIE MOSIMANN

Makes 6 servings

Prep Time: 30 minutes *Standing and Cooling Times: 45-60 minutes*
Chilling Time: 3-8 hours

Blood oranges are available in the late fall and winter and, as you can guess, are dark red. This easy and light dessert makes quite the show.

1¼ teaspoons unflavored gelatin
¼ cup milk
1¼ cups heavy (whipping) cream
⅓ cup sugar
¼ teaspoon salt
¼ vanilla bean, split
1¼ cups buttermilk
¼ cup sour cream
3 blood oranges
¼-⅓ cup orange juice, if needed
1 Tablespoon lemon juice
¾ teaspoon unflavored gelatin
¼ cup sugar

1. For the Panna Cotta, soften 1¼ teaspoons gelatin in ¼ cup milk for 5 minutes.
2. Combine the cream, ⅓ cup sugar, and salt in a saucepan.
3. Scrape in the seeds from ¼ of a vanilla bean. Add the ¼ pod to the cream.
4. Bring the cream to a simmer, stirring to dissolve the sugar.
5. Allow to stand for 30 minutes. Then strain into a clean large bowl.
6. Stir in the gelatin mixture, stirring until it is fully dissolved.
7. Let cool to room temperature.
8. In a separate bowl, stir the buttermilk and sour cream together.
9. Whisk the buttermilk and sour cream mixture into the gelatin mixture.
10. This makes 3 cups of liquid. Pour into 6 martini glasses that have been placed at an angle. (Put a plate on a tray. Set the martini glasses at an angle on the edge of the plate.) Chill until set.
11. Meanwhile, make the gelée by cutting the oranges in half. Cut a ⅛-inch-thick slice from the center of each orange half. Set them aside for garnishing later.
12. Squeeze oranges for juice. If they do not give a total of ¾ cup of juice, add regular orange juice to equal ¾ cup.
13. Strain the orange juice into a small saucepan.
14. Remove 1 tablespoon of juice and mix it with the lemon juice in a small bowl. Sprinkle ¾ teaspoon gelatin over it and set aside.
15. Heat ¼ cup sugar and remaining blood orange juice until it starts to steam. Do not boil. Stir to dissolve the sugar completely.
16. Remove from the heat and add the gelatin mixture. Stir to dissolve.
17. Cool this gelée completely to room temperature. Then pour over the set Panna Cotta.
18. Chill for several hours or overnight.
19. Garnish each glass with the reserved orange slices before serving.

Vanilla or Maple Custard

DANIELLE HANSCOM THODE

Makes 1½ cups

Prep Time: 45 minutes ✂ *Cooling Time: 20-30 minutes*

big bowl of ice

4 large egg yolks

¼ cup granulated sugar only if making Vanilla Custard

¼ cup maple syrup only if making Maple Custard

¼ teaspoon fine sea salt

1 cup half-and-half

½ Tablespoon vanilla only if making Vanilla Custard

Both flavorings are delicious. This is the custard we pour over our Little Brown Bettys and use to make our Trifles.

1. Fill a large bowl with ice. The bowl should be large enough to hold the top of a double boiler. Set the bowl with ice aside.
2. Add a quart of water to the bottom part of a double boiler, making sure the water will not touch the bottom of the top pan when it's suspended overhead. Heat the water to simmering.
3. Whisk together the egg yolks, sugar or maple syrup, and sea salt in the top of the double boiler (off the heat) until well blended.
4. In a small saucepan, bring the half-and-half to a boil. Remove from the heat and let it cool slightly.
5. Very slowly pour the hot half-and-half over the yolks, whisking vigorously. You want to avoid having the yolks curdle.
6. Place the top of the double boiler over the hot pan of water. Whisk the mixture constantly until its temperature reaches 165°. You have to stick with it!
7. Immediately remove from the heat. Stir in the vanilla only if you're making Vanilla Custard. Set the filled top of the double boiler into the bowl of ice.
8. Keep whisking until the custard is completely cool, about 30 minutes.
9. Strain through a fine meshed sieve into a container with a lid. Before closing the lid, press a piece of plastic wrap on top of the custard to prevent a skin from forming. Close the lid and refrigerate until you're ready to use it, up to three days.

Proof Is In the Pudding

This Tops It All

Blueberry Sauce

ELLEN GUTMAN CHENAUX

Serves 12

Prep Time: 5 minutes ❧ *Cooking Time: 3-5 minutes*

2 cups blueberries
(if frozen, thawed)

1 cup sugar

juice of half a lemon

1 Tablespoon cornstarch

1 Tablespoon orange,
or lemon, juice

1. Combine blueberries, sugar, and juice from half a lemon in a medium saucepan.
2. In a glass custard cup, mix cornstarch with the 1 Tablespoon orange or lemon juice, stirring to eliminate any lumps. Set aside.
3. Bring the berry mixture to a soft boil over medium heat. Stir in the cornstarch mixture carefully.
4. Continue cooking, stirring until the sauce is thickened.

Over pancakes, mixed with oatmeal, or a topping for ice cream, this sauce is a keeper.

This Tops It All

Hot Fudge Sauce: The World's Easiest

LYNNETTE SCOFIELD

Makes one cup

Prep time: 2 minutes *Cooking Time: 5 minutes*

6-oz. package really good chocolate chips

5⅓-oz. can evaporated milk

½ teaspoon vanilla

1. Using a microwave-safe bowl (I use a four-cup glass measuring cup) place the chips and milk in the bowl.
2. Microwave for 30-second increments.
3. Stir after each 30-second increment.
4. Continue to microwave until the mixture becomes smooth and creamy.
5. Stir in vanilla.
6. Store in the fridge.

This is such an easy and fast hot fudge sauce and, I'll admit, is even good cold. Don't ask how I would know.

Yogurt Sauce with Lime & Ginger

LYNNETTE SCOFIELD

Makes 6 healthy servings

Prep Time: 10 minutes

1 cup vanilla Greek yogurt

1 Tablespoon finely diced candied ginger

1 Tablespoon lime zest

1. Combine all ingredients gently.
2. Store in the fridge.
3. Serve it chilled.

At the inn, we served a lot of melon, and this really enhanced its flavor. Try it, too, on blueberries for a delicious dessert. The sauce itself is flavorful, and I love how easily you can reduce or increase the amount of any of the ingredients according to your taste preferences.

This Tops It All

Vanilla Sauce

DEBBIE MOSIMANN

Makes 1½ cups

Prep Time: 10 minutes ❧ *Cooking Time: 3-5 minutes*

1 cup water

⅔ cup sugar

1 Tablespoon cornstarch

pinch of salt

2 Tablespoons (¼ stick) butter, cut in pieces

2 teaspoons vanilla—really good vanilla!

1. Bring the water to a boil.
2. In a small bowl combine the sugar, cornstarch, and salt.
3. Whisk the sugar-cornstarch mixture into the hot water. Bring to a full boil, stirring constantly until it thickens.
4. Remove from the heat. Whisk in the butter and vanilla until the butter melts.
5. Serve warm.

This sauce goes well with, oh, so many things. . . French toast and bread puddings, just to mention two. My mom always served it with her steamed Christmas pudding.

This Tops It All

Bourbon Sauce

DEBBIE MOSIMANN

Makes: 1¾ cups

Prep Time: 5 minutes ✿ *Cooking Time: 5 minutes*

1 Tablespoon cornstarch

½ cup brown sugar

1 cup cream

½ cup whole milk

pinch of salt

4 Tablespoons butter
(half a stick), cut in slices

¼ cup bourbon, *or*
whiskey, brandy, *or* rum

1. Whisk the cornstarch and sugar together in a saucepan.
2. Combine the cream, milk, and salt with the sugar and cornstarch. Turn heat to medium, whisking the ingredients until smooth. Bring to a boil.
3. Remove from the heat. Whisk in the butter and then the bourbon.
4. Serve warm.

This is absolutely delicious with Cinnamon Bread Pudding.

Homemade Caramel Sauce

DEBBIE MOSIMANN

Makes: 1½ cups

Prep Time: 15 minutes ❧ *Cooling Time: 10 minutes*

1 cup sugar

1 Tablespoon corn syrup

¼ cup boiling water

¾ cup heavy cream, heated to scalding

2 Tablespoons (¼ stick) butter, sliced

½ teaspoon salt

1 teaspoon vanilla

1. In a large, heavy saucepan combine the sugar, corn syrup, and water.
2. Use a candy thermometer to monitor the temperature. You're aiming for about 330-340°. Please note: That is very hot!
3. Bring to a boil, watching closely until the syrup turns a deep amber but is not burned. That's around the 340° mark.
4. Carefully and slowly add the hot cream. The mixture will spritz and splatter.
5. Stir until well combined. Then turn off the heat. Do not continue to boil because you do not want to reduce the mixture.
6. Remove from the heat. Stir in the butter and salt.
7. Allow to cool 10 minutes. Then stir in the vanilla.
8. When the sauce has reached room temperature, refrigerate it until you're ready for it.
9. When ready to use the sauce, gently heat it in the microwave if you wish.

I love caramel stirred into coffee or hot chocolate, drizzled over cheesecake topped with apples, drizzled over baked apples, combined with cream cheese, crème fraiche or mascarpone, and used as a dip for pears.
Or just as is!

Caramel is one of my favorite flavors. This sauce is also good over ice cream, puddings, poached pears, chocolate cake, and sundaes. You can even fold it into whipped cream for a very special topping.

This Tops It All

Glazed Bananas

KATHRYN WHITE

Makes 4 servings

Prep Time: 10 minutes   ✥   *Cooking Time: 4 minutes*

4 Tablespoons (half a stick) butter

1 cup brown sugar

4 bananas, peeled and sliced in chunks

½ teaspoon cinnamon, *optional*

¼ teaspoon nutmeg, *optional*

whipped cream, *optional*

1. Melt butter in a skillet (non-stick is best) and add the brown sugar. Turn the heat up to medium-high and melt the sugar, stirring with a spoon to combine. Watch the heat and turn it down as needed so the sugar doesn't scorch.
2. Add the banana chunks and cook about 1 minute, using the spoon to toss the bananas in the sugar mixture.
3. Sprinkle with cinnamon and/or nutmeg, if you wish.
4. Serve the bananas on top of ice cream or your favorite pound cake. Or serve them on plates topped with whipped cream.

This is a super-easy topping and dessert to make and enjoy.

Crème Fraiche

KRISTIE ROSSET

Makes 10 servings
Prep Time: 2 minutes

1 cup sour cream

¼ cup heavy cream

¼ cup brown sugar

½ teaspoon vanilla

1. Whisk the ingredients together in a small bowl until well blended.
2. Refrigerate until ready to use. Keeps well up to 2 weeks.

Buttermilk Glaze

KATHRYN WHITE

Makes enough to glaze a 13 × 9-inch cake, or a cake baked in a tube or Bundt pan.
Prep Time: 5 minutes  *Cooking Time: 7-10 minutes*

1 cup sugar

½ teaspoon baking soda

½ cup buttermilk

4 Tablespoons (half a stick) butter, cut in pieces

1 Tablespoon light corn syrup

1 teaspoon vanilla

1. In a small saucepan over medium-high temperature, combine sugar, baking soda, buttermilk, butter, and corn syrup. Bring to a boil while stirring occasionally.
2. Continue cooking for 5 minutes.
3. Remove from the heat. Stir in vanilla. Spread over cake while still slightly warm.

This Tops It All

Chocolate Gravy

KRISTIE ROSSET

Makes 6 servings

Prep Time: 5 minutes 🌸 *Cook Time: 5 minutes*

8 Tablespoons (1 stick) butter

4 Tablespoons unsweetened cocoa powder

4 Tablespoons flour

¾ cup sugar

2 cups milk

1. Melt the butter in a small saucepan. Add the cocoa powder and flour, whisking until well combined.
2. Stir in the sugar and milk, whisking constantly.
3. Cook over medium heat, continuing to whisk until thickened to gravy consistency.
4. Allow to cool. Serve over your choice of pastry or fruit.

This surprisingly tasty treat is an old Southern country recipe from my son-in-law's family. Top biscuits, pound cake, or a bowl of strawberries with this gravy!

Cream Cheese Frosting

KATHRYN WHITE

*Makes enough for one 13 × 9-inch cake,
2 dozen cupcakes, or one two-layer cake*

Prep Time: 5 minutes

8 ounces cream cheese, softened to room temperature

4 Tablespoons (half a stick) butter, softened to room temperature

1-lb. box confectioners sugar

1 teaspoon vanilla

1 Tablespoon milk (more or less) to vary consistency

1. Combine cream cheese and butter in a medium bowl. Using a hand mixer, blend on medium speed until well mixed.
2. Stir in the confectioners sugar and vanilla. Beat on high until light and fluffy.
3. Add a little milk if needed for spreading.
4. Spread on the cooled cake.

Note: You can cover and refrigerate this frosting for several days.

This is most often used with carrot cake, but thinned a bit with milk, it can be drizzled on pound cakes and cakes baked in a Bundt or tube pan.

This Tops It All

Salud, Cheers, L'chaim, Prost, Salute

Strawberry Basil Lemonade

DEBBIE MOSIMANN

Makes 12 cups

Prep Time: 15 minutes

8 cups warm water

1¾ cups sugar

1 pint fresh strawberries

3-4 stems basil, leaves only, sliced in ¼-inch-wide strips

1 Tablespoon sugar

1½ cups fresh lemon juice

2 lemon slices

1. In a bowl or pitcher combine the water and 1¾ cups sugar, stirring until the sugar is dissolved.
2. Stem and halve the strawberries. Put them into a large pitcher, along with the basil leaves and the 1 Tablespoon sugar.
3. Mash the strawberries while at the same time bruising the basil to release its flavor. Do not over-mash; you still want chunks of strawberry.
4. Add the lemon juice and the sweetened water. Stir.
5. Add the lemon slices.
6. Serve over ice.

A different refreshing drink for those hot summer days. Genovese basil is perfect for this and grows easily in a sunny spot.

Berry Smoothie

KRISTIE ROSSET

Makes 1 serving
Prep Time: 5 minutes

half a banana, frozen *or* fresh

1 cup organic frozen fruit of your choice

1 Tablespoon peanut butter powder, *optional*

2 teaspoons organic chia seeds

1 cup unsweetened vanilla almond milk, *or* other milk of your choosing

1. Put all ingredients into a blender.
2. Set the blender to the "smoothie" or medium setting, and blend away. It may take a couple of stirs and spins at this setting.
3. Pour into a glass, and enjoy a healthy, refreshing breakfast.

Like many of you, I am using less meat in my diet and increasing plant-based foods. This fruit smoothie is satisfying for breakfast and sustains me for hours. For a more complete breakfast, I add a handful of nuts after enjoying the smoothie. Incorporate any frozen fruit, including over-ripe bananas. Just slice bananas into bite-size pieces and freeze packets containing half-a-banana each. Using frozen bananas and frozen fruit eliminates the need for ice or sweeteners.

Note: I add peanut butter powder for additional protein; however, when I use higher protein almond milk (such as the almond-cashew-pea protein), I eliminate the peanut powder. Unfortunately, not all stores carry the high protein milk.

Salud, Cheers, L'chaim, Prost, Salute

8 Broads Classic Lemon Drop Martinis

DEBBIE MOSIMANN AND JOYCE SCHULTE

Makes 1 serving
Prep Time: 5 minutes

1½ ounce Citroen vodka, *or*, if you like a more spirit-forward version, use 2 ounces of vodka

½ ounce limoncello

1 ounce fresh lemon juice

¼ ounce simple syrup

ice

1 lemon slice

1. Chill your martini glasses by filling them with ice and water. Let them stand at least 5 minutes. Or just keep a couple of glasses in the freezer all the time.
2. Measure and pour all the ingredients into a cocktail shaker.
3. Add ice and shake well.
4. Pour into a chilled martini glass.
5. Top with a thin slice of lemon, or a lemon wedge, on the side of the glass, and serve.

Whenever the 8 Broads are together, we inevitably turn one night to making lemon drop martinis. They're especially a favorite of Joyce's and Deb's. Joyce errs on the tart side; Debbie likes a sweeter taste. We all agree that you must use Citroen (lemon) vodka, or the drink is just not a lemon drop! We have tried different recipes over the years, but this one is the most pleasing to all 8 of us. It's our classic. We hope you enjoy it and have as much fun and laughter with it as we have had over the years.

Angel's Tip

LYNNETTE SCOFIELD

Makes 1 serving

Prep Time: 2 minutes

¾ ounce crème de cacao

¾ ounce heavy cream

1. Pour crème de cacao into the bottom of a cordial glass.
2. Top off with cream.
3. Sip and enjoy.

If you grew up in the 1950s, you know this was a very popular drink. My mother would make one of these and let us "have a sip."

Dark Rum Mojitos

KRISTIE ROSSET

Makes 1 serving

Prep Time: 5 minutes

6-8 fresh mint leaves

juice of half a lime

2 teaspoons brown sugar

crushed ice

2 ounces dark Cuban rum

soda water

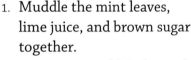

1. Muddle the mint leaves, lime juice, and brown sugar together.
2. Pour into an old-fashioned glass.
3. Add the dark rum, crushed ice, and soda water to top off the glass. Stir and serve.

During one September, several of the 8 Broads attended an informative and fun Select Registry Innkeeping Conference in Key West. Were we surprised that September is the hottest month in Key West! Staying for a few days after the conference, we enjoyed lazing around the small pool of our friends' beautiful home. Following extremely busy summer months, we innkeepers needed a break! One day, my husband, Ray, happily volunteered to be our "cabana boy," bringing freshly made mojitos and lunch to us. It was a wonderful day! We supremely enjoyed not only each other's company, but also being treated to such fine service.

These mojitos taste best when they're served to you with joy while you're relaxing in and around a pool!

Cranberry Liqueur for Cosmopolitans

YVONNE MARTIN

Makes 5–6 cups liqueur

Prep Time: 10 minutes *Standing Time: 3 weeks*

2 cups sugar

1 cup water

2 cups fresh cranberries

26-oz. bottle vodka

1. You will need one or two large mason jars with lids—either two one-quart jars, or one-half gallon jar. Wash and sanitize the jar(s).
2. Mix the sugar and water in a medium saucepan. Bring to a simmer, stirring until the sugar dissolves.
3. Chop the cranberries fine using a food processor. Stir into the syrup.
4. Pour the cranberry mixture into jar(s). Stir in the vodka and mix well.
5. Put lids on the jars and store in a cool dark place. Shake the mixture every day.
6. After 3 weeks, strain the liquid and discard the cranberries.
7. Pour the liqueur into clean bottles or mason jars. It's best to store this in the fridge.

Cosmopolitans

Makes 2 drinks

½ cup cranberry liqueur

¼ cup Triple Sec, *or* Cointreau

2 Tablespoons lime juice

ice

1. Shake in a cocktail shaker with ice.
2. Pour into martini glasses. Cheers!

For a lighter and more refreshing summer drink, pour into a tall glass with ice and top up with club soda.

Those Crazy 8s!

ELLEN GUTMAN CHENAUX

Makes 2 servings

Prep Time: 5 minutes

1 cup rosé wine

1 cup club soda

¼ cup Campari

½ cup limoncello

juice of half a lemon

a few dashes of
orange bitters

ice

2 lemon slices

2 fresh strawberries

1. Stir wine, club soda, Campari, limoncello, fresh lemon juice, and bitters together in a pitcher.
2. Place ice in 2 glasses. Pour mixture over ice, and then garnish each with a lemon slice and a strawberry.

The 8 Broads taste-tested this libation and have declared it a winner! With thanks to Peter Chenaux and Kelsey Morrison.

Espresso Martinis

DEBBIE MOSIMANN

Makes 2 small servings
Prep Time: 5 minutes

lots of ice

2 small martini glasses

2 shots espresso

1½ shots vanilla vodka

½ shot Kahlua, *or* any
good coffee liqueur

½ shot Godiva dark liquor

½ shot Godiva white liquor

1 shot cream, *or*
half and half

1. Fill the martini glasses with ice and then water to chill.
2. Fill a martini shaker with ice. Add the espresso, vodka, coffee liqueur, both Godiva liquors, and the cream.
3. Cover and shake vigorously! You want foam.
4. Empty the chilled glasses. Using a strainer, fill the martini glasses with the yummy espresso martini and enjoy.

The first time I had an espresso martini was in Chicago and I fell in love. I watched the bartender craft them and came home determined to get the same results. After many tries and help from a local bartender, I am happy with this beautiful, delicious dessert drink! Decaf espresso is fine.

Hot Mulled Wine

DANIELLE HANSCOM THODE

Makes 4 servings
Prep Time: 15 minutes

2 oranges, well scrubbed and cut into ¼-inch-thick slices, about 6 per orange

1 bottle of red wine*

4 sticks cinnamon

2 star anise

3 Tablespoons honey (I use a raw, unfiltered honey)

⅓ cup Grand Marnier

* I use a Malbec. In other words, choose a decent wine, nothing crazy expensive, but not a cheap bottle of red either.

1. Reserve the 4 nicest orange slices and set them aside.
2. Place the wine, cinnamon sticks, star anise, honey, and 8 orange slices in a large, non-reactive saucepan.
3. Bring to a boil over high heat. Immediately reduce to a simmer. Simmer for 5 minutes.
4. Remove from heat. Remove the cooked orange slices and star anise.
5. Stir in the Grand Marnier.
6. Place one cinnamon stick in each of 4 wine glasses. Evenly distribute the mulled wine among the glasses. Decorate each one with a reserved slice of orange. Serve warm.

Note: You can easily double or triple this recipe.

A delicious and grown-up treat for the holidays. In German they call this Glühwein, or "glow wine." It will give your cheeks a lovely glow by your second or third glass!

Salud, Cheers, L'chaim, Prost, Salute

French Hot Chocolate

DEBBIE MOSIMANN

Makes 8-10 servings

Prep Time: 15 minutes ✂ *Chilling Time: 30-60 minutes*

1 cup whipping cream

1 cup good quality dark chocolate pieces

1 Tablespoon unsweetened cocoa powder

1 Tablespoon water

4 cups milk, heated almost to scalding

1. In a non-reactive pan, heat the whipping cream to just under boiling.
2. Place the chocolate into a bowl. Pour the hot cream over the chocolate. Stir to melt. This is a traditional ganache.
3. In a small bowl, combine the cocoa powder and water. Then stir into the chocolate mixture.
4. Allow to cool 10 minutes, then place in the refrigerator for about 20-50 minutes. The mixture should not be hard, but it should be set.
5. When ready to serve, use the whisk attachment of your mixer to whip the chocolate for 4-5 minutes, until it reaches a smooth, frosting-like consistency.
6. Spoon about 3 Tablespoons of the chocolate into heat-proof glasses or small mugs.
7. Pour hot milk over top. Stir gently and serve.

This is a different way to make hot chocolate, but it turns into such a rich, creamy drink that you will never look back. You can hold the chocolate mix in the refrigerator, but bring it to room temperature before using it.

Index

C

D

E

Frangelica Chocolate Silk Pie, 194

N

M

O

S

Strawberry Basil Lemonade, 228

Meet the Eight Broads in the Kitchen!

Ellen Gutman Chenaux

Among the eight of us, I am known as "The Pie Broad." My passion for baking didn't start with the usual suspects like my mom or grandmothers, but rather with my dad. His sweet tooth and my Betty Crocker cooking set. Baking those bite-size cakes for him taught me how very satisfying it is to bake for others. What a yummy way to communicate love! I soon graduated to "real" desserts, particularly pastries, and even a croquembouche for 60. I have retired from innkeeping after 17 years (Birchwood Inn, Lenox, Massachusetts), but my passion for desserts—baking and eating them—lives on.

Yvonne Martin

I lived my early years in a tiny town in Scotland, spending much of my childhood with my grandmother. She and her two neighbors all vied for first-place prizes for their baked goods and preserves at the local fair and church bazaars. They also raised much of their own food. I credit those three ladies with teaching me to cook, bake, and appreciate local fresh food.

When I was 12, my family emigrated to Canada, where I grew up, met my husband, Ian, in college, and went on to work in investments and finance. Following a life-changing event, we both decided to leave corporate life. In 1992, we took the helm as innkeepers of The White Oak Inn in Danville, Ohio. As an innkeeper I've had plenty of opportunity to hone my cooking skills for appreciative audiences, always ready to sample the results.

Debbie Mosimann

I grew up in a farmers-market-going family, learning about great food early on. Time in Austria and Switzerland expanded and defined my love of baking and cooking. Innkeeping at Swiss Woods, Lititz, Pennsylvania, for 33 years has provided the perfect setting for me to create and experiment, serving guests with a variety of new flavors mixed with the traditional. Local cooking classes have provided me with an avenue for passing on what I have learned, along with my continuing enthusiasm to create. My family includes four children, five grandchildren, and a husband, all of whom enjoy taste-testing everything I make.

Kristie Rosset

Of all the things I do in the kitchen, baking is my absolute favorite. From the first time I tasted cookie dough as a little girl, I was hooked and have loved baking ever since. To this day I still bring homemade cookies to my grandchildren's many games and meets, enough for the entire team. Now retired from the inn we created (Lookout Point Lakeside Inn, Hot Springs, Arkansas), we find great joy in sharing delicious meals and desserts with beloved family and friends. Ray and I love to travel, savoring local cuisines from around the globe and bringing home new culinary ideas.

Joyce Schulte

Great food was the cornerstone of our inn, the Chambered Nautilus Bed and Breakfast in Seattle, Washington. As a retired innkeeper for several years, I am still in Seattle and still in love with the Pacific Northwest. I absolutely continue to love food, cooking, and sharing it with friends at tables filled with laughter and fun. Many of my friends are great cooks, and as I've always said, "My favorite meal is one that has been prepared for me by someone else!"

Lynnette Scofield

Every year when I attended a conference for innkeepers, I came home with great new ideas. And then came the Atlanta conference, when I was invited to become one of the 8 Broads in the Kitchen. Life changed! It's amazing how our group of eight has jelled together around great ideas, fun times, and wonderful food. I am thrilled to be one of the Broads.

Twenty years as owner and innkeeper of The William Henry Miller Inn in Ithaca, New York, have flown by, and I'm so grateful for the privilege of cooking and baking for wonderful guests. We so hope that you enjoy our cookbook and share the joy that we feel.

Danielle Hanscom Thode

Growing up in Switzerland in a family of food-lovers, I learned the craft of cooking and entertaining at an early age. My late husband, Michael, and I were the innkeepers of the Brampton Inn in Chestertown, Maryland, for more than 30 years, where I honed my skills. To this day there is no greater joy in my life than to share a good glass of wine and a home-cooked meal with family, friends, and the other 7 Broads!

Kathryn White

Food and music reveal the soul in all of us, and nothing gives me more pleasure than baking and cooking for others. Operating The Beechmont Inn, Hanover, Pennsylvania, for 15 years as an award-winning innkeeper, I relish having guests in my home and delivering fresh-from-the-oven baked goodies to friends. Food is a way to say welcome, and I love to stay around the table for conversation and laughs. I remain active in the innkeeping industry as a consultant, I love to travel, and I am passionate about opera.

BREAKFAST & BRUNCH RECIPES

from 8 Innkeepers of Notable Bed & Breakfasts

Get this other delicious cookbook from the 8 Broads!

Try these matchless 150 dishes from *Breakfast & Brunch Recipes*, also from the 8 Broads, including:

- **Parmesan Heirloom Cherry Tomatoes**

- **Blueberry Sour Cream Pancakes with Lemon Sauce**

- **Caramelized Onion Omelets**

- **Apricot Chocolate Crumb Squares**

Each recipe includes Prep Time and Cooking Time—along with easy-to-follow, step-by-step instructions and full-color photography.

Available wherever books are sold.